D1032681

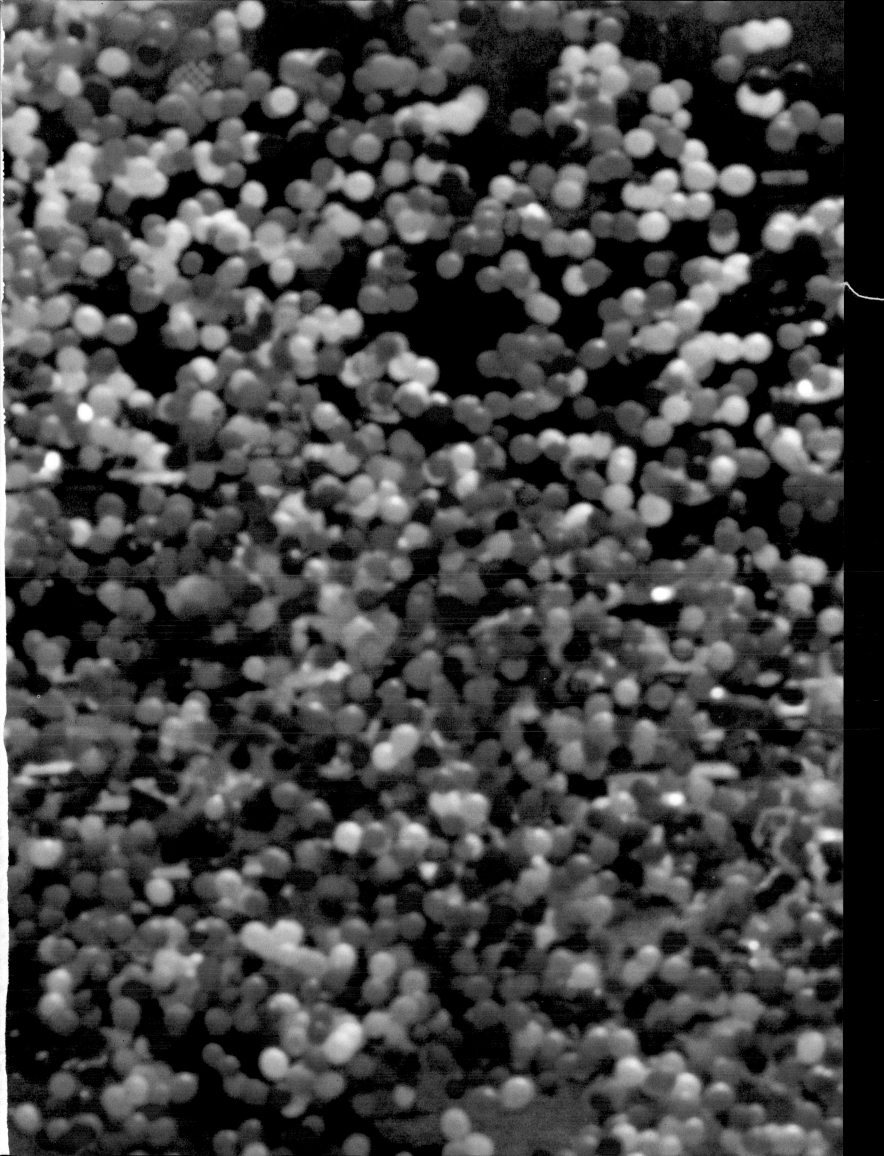

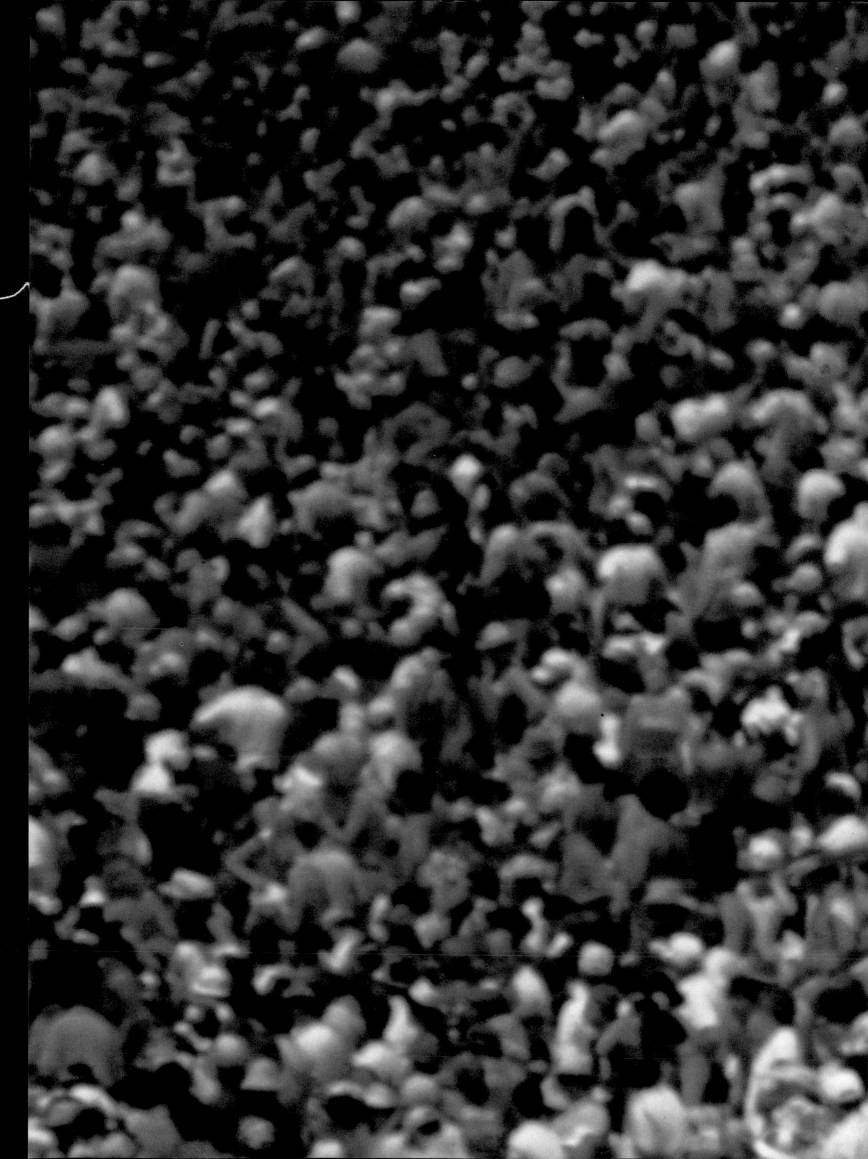

A Great American Tradition

INDY

More Than a Race

500

by Tom Carnegie

McGraw-Hill Book Company

New York   St. Louis   San Francisco   Auckland   Bogotá   Hamburg
Johannesburg   London   Madrid   Milan   Mexico   Montreal   New Delhi
Panama   Paris   São Paulo   Singapore   Sydney   Tokyo   Toronto

Data

ce.   I. Title.
ed.
          796.7′2′06877252

by Dai Nippon, Tokyo, Japan
Type Inc., Syracuse, New York

used with permission of the Indianapolis Motor
orporation.

A Chanticleer Press Edition

Created and designed by Massimo Vignelli and Gudrun Buettner

Developed and edited by Jane Opper

Foreword by Patrick Bedard

Captions by Ted West

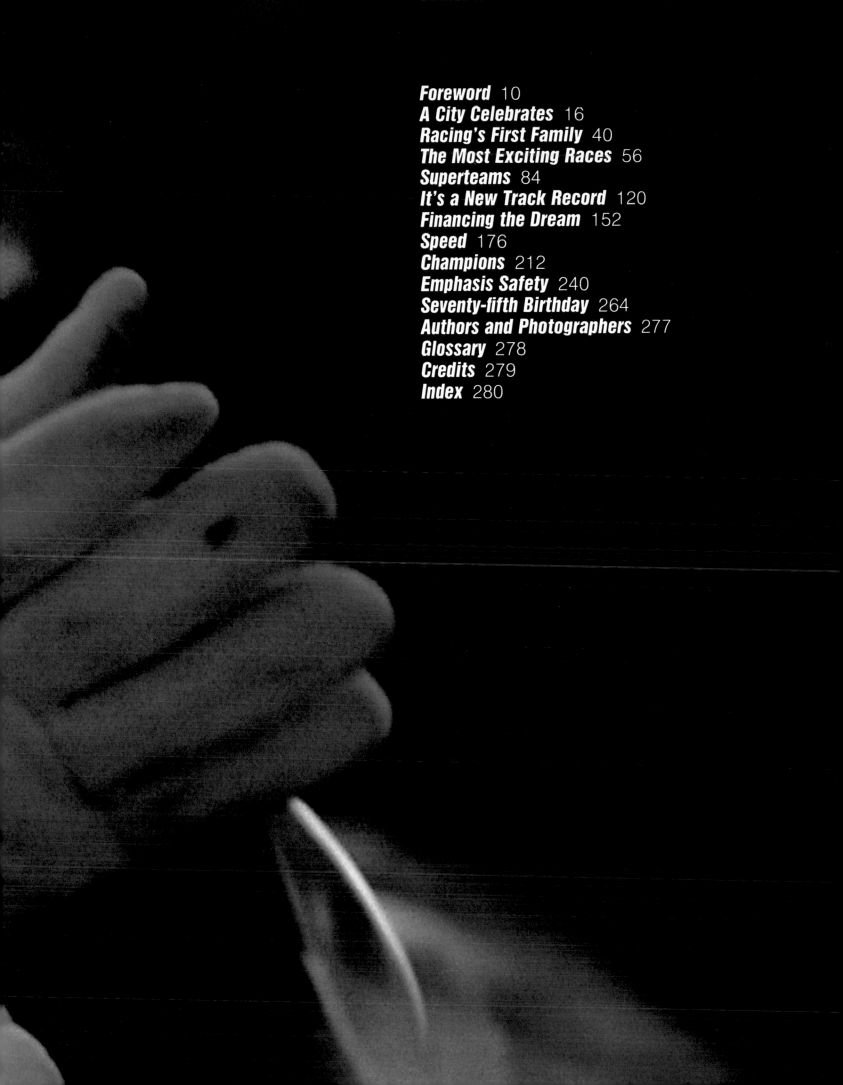

Contents

As a farm kid growing up in Iowa, I learned the prairie way of choosing words for their literal meaning and speaking them with a flat accent, and if someone had suggested that Everest loomed large over the flatlands of Indiana, I would have found this sense of geography woefully deficient. But the years since have brought understanding of metaphor, and now Everest is my mind's top-drawer impression of the Indianapolis 500. Moreover, this mind has concluded that any lesser image constitutes a failure to understand.

I know many people who think of Indy as simply another automobile race. Even as a farm kid, I was never guilty of such gross oversimplification. Just another race would not have found its way out over the radio in the middle of Memorial Day, and just another race would not have drawn the attention of grown men such as my father who had no time for inconsequential pastimes like baseball and fishing.

I always knew the Indianapolis 500 had to be some exceptional occurrence, and for a long time I assumed that its stature rested on the simple fact that it was the most dangerous undertaking a man could face short of war. This assumption stuck, even as I grew to adulthood and began driving slow cars in short races with such ardor that, after each event, recalling my name was an iffy proposition.

Racing became a passion, and I yielded to it every spare minute and many that weren't spare, but I never confused what I did on the track with the way Indy racers drive. I was using the car to explore my own limits and to gauge myself against others in similar cars: Speed was our measure. Indy drivers, on the other hand, were obviously gambling with the fates. The Indianapolis Motor Speedway was the Big Casino, and it held no attraction for me.

The understanding of metaphor comes slowly, but it comes. Did you know that the Indianapolis 500 is the oldest auto race in the world, run every year since 1911 except for two years during World War I and four years during World War II? The 2.5-mile track today is the same rectangular circuit that was carved into Indiana farm country in 1909, with the same ⅝-mile long straights and the same ⅛-mile short straights connected by the same four ¼-mile turns banked at nine degrees, twelve minutes. The 500 has grown to become the largest one-day sporting event in the world, seating more than . . . well, Speedway management won't say exactly how many, but the 500 generates revenues substantial enough so that the track, now a valuable piece of real estate encircled by metropolitan Indianapolis, can lie fallow the rest of the year. Clearly, the Indianapolis 500 is now important enough so that its date is inked on to the world's calendar of events.

As a writer on assignment, I met with Speedway historian Bob Laycock, and through his notes and files and stories I began to see how the 500 has been inked on to the calendars of so many racers, too. In the early days, they came from all across America by car and by train. They came from Europe by steamship. The entry logs include some of the world's most noted drivers: Barney Oldfield and Ralph DePalma and Rene Thomas and Jimmy Murphy. They were joined by the great minds of automotive design: the Duesenberg brothers and the Chevrolet brothers and Harry Miller. Once each year, they brought their skills and their inventions to the 2.5-mile rectangle in Indianapolis, Indiana, where the object was speed. Each year they challenged old limits, and their new accomplishments were duly recorded: above 100 mph for the first time in 1919, above 125 mph in 1937, above 150 mph in 1962, above 200 mph in 1977. The numbers change with time, but the challenge remains the same: man against the 2.5-mile rectangle.

The men who made the breakthroughs are now famous, but Laycock told equally enthralling stories about those who never quite broke the bonds of obscurity; men who tried and died young, men who mortgaged the house every spring to get a stake, men who drove racing cars because it was better than working, men who tried to break into the elite thirty-three-car starting field year after year and finally reached their goal—or never reached it. As I listened to him talk, an image took shape in my mind, and as it hardened around the edges I could see it was the metaphor. Since very nearly the beginning of automotive time, drivers from around the world have been measuring themselves against the Speedway, and except for having its original brick surface paved over with asphalt, the 2.5-mile rectangle has not changed. Here is the enduring arbiter of skill, the driver's Everest. The same challenge Ray Harroun, the first 500 winner, took up in 1911 could be taken up today.

Could I climb this Everest? What I had once regarded as a festival of risk, based on the accounts of newsmen, had become the supreme measure of a driver's ability when described by historian Laycock. Although I had driven in only minor-league races, I had done well, too well to have any sense of my limits. I yearned for the definitive test. Could I climb this driver's Everest? I had to try.

If reaching the summit translates to winning the 500, then my climb did not get far, but I did qualify for the race twice and I have done enough laps over 200 mph to be completely comfortable with the idea. Comfortable? Perhaps that is not exactly the right word, but I did find joy in the speed, and in saying so I may be revealing the alteration of mind one undergoes in the transformation to Indy driver. Speed becomes everything. Speed becomes the only thing, that and keeping the pieces intact so that more speed can be pursued on the morrow, and when more speed comes it spreads a grin across the face behind the helmet. It's common to cite the bravery, heroism and instantaneous reflexes of Indy drivers and assume that those are the qualities that separate these individuals from other achievers in this world. Maybe, but in my opinion it's the grin that comes with speed, which is certainly a rarer endowment.

The modern Indy car is more aircraft than automobile, more missile than aircraft, a projectile of neatly joined aluminum, magnesium and carbon fiber, thrust forward by a shrieking burner of methanol. To encounter one for the first time and to find your name painted on its side is to confront free will square in the face. You don't have to get in if you don't want to. The cockpit is shoulder width, narrower at the hips. You wear the car like an alloy G-suit and it takes you to a realm where the road's curves produce pain, your brain kicks into hyperspeed, and the man becomes utterly self-reliant. It is a place that has never been described convincingly.

Anything that burns like a rocket does not burn for long, however, and Indy drivers spend most of the month of May walking around on terra firma, citizens of the Speedway just like everybody else in Gasoline Alley, while their exotic cars are endlessly rebuilt, refueled, readjusted and refined. For every minute in the other realm, there's an hour of waiting, time to absorb the pageantry that unfolds within the Indy Speedway every May.

The racers come and go like migratory creatures, but the Speedway and its many personnel are constant, enduring, unchanging. I liked that. Everests shouldn't change. But there is one thing about the Speedway people I appreciate even more than their constancy: They choose their words with restraint and speak them with flat accents; to the Iowa farm boy now displaced from his roots, they sound very much like old neighbors. Indianapolis is middle America, and the 500 remains a middle-American jamboree.

Tom Carnegie is so much a part of the Speedway I almost think of him as infrastructure. We've had so many conversations, and his choice of words always delighted my middle-American ear. But frankly, his delivery resonates like Zeus and I always suspected that he was from somewhere else, just trying to fit in amongst middle Americans because he overflows with humanity and he thought that would make us more comfortable. Only recently did I discover that he grew up in Missouri. And now that I think of it, Everest's announcer should have a voice that rolls like thunder, so my last reservation about Tom Carnegie has been lifted.

As a rookie, I came to think of Tom Carnegie as the voice of ratification. Qualifying is an Indianapolis ritual that must be satisfied. The rookie, to assume the rank of Indy driver, must perform four laps at an average speed quick enough to rank in the top thirty-three. The track goes still for qualifying. Everything goes quiet, except for one thrusting engine and one booming voice. I've heard it so many times. "Heeezzzzzz on it!" as the car rushes off the fourth turn to take the green flag. Then the car orbits out of earshot, leaving only the voice of Tom Carnegie to track its progress and bear witness to its accomplishment.

I have seen the green myself, through vision made blurry by buffeting winds, and I've clenched against the forces and heard the tires scratch for traction against the pavement and feared that something untoward might take away my chance. And I've seen smiles of friends and crew when I returned to the pits and felt their approbation. Yet the act always seems incomplete, lacking the final ratification, because I only felt it. I never heard the voice of Tom Carnegie boom out his running commentary over the PA. Such is the significance of his words.

A man like that should write a book, and finally he has.

Patrick Bedard

Acknowledgments
The writer gratefully acknowledges the valued technical
insight of Jim McGee and Peter Gibbons of Patrick Racing,
Mark Bridges of Machinists, and Dennis Hardy and Phil Casey
of Team Cotter. I would also like to thank Al Bloemker, Vice-
President of the Indianapolis Motor Speedway, for his
guidance in historical matters; Jerry Chapman of WRTV
for his encouragement, and the Speedway Public Address
team for making every month of May enjoyable. Betty Allen's
support is greatly appreciated, as is Bob Laycock's research.

To my dear family, D. J., Blair, Charlotte and Robert

A City Celebrates

In some places the first sign of spring is an adventurous robin. At Indianapolis, it's the arrival of race fan Larry Bisceglia. Early in April, Larry pulls his trusty Ford van up to Gate Three along Hulman Boulevard and West Sixteenth Street. It's the signal for Indianapolis to start the annual Speedway celebration. Always the first in line, Larry eats, sleeps and lives on the Speedway grounds for the proverbial forty days and forty nights in order to be the first to enter the track.

Larry has made the 1,900-mile pilgrimage from his home in Yuma, Arizona, every year since 1949. At first Larry drove a 1933 DeSoto, replacing it in 1959 with a 1951 Chevy van. In 1958 the Speedway presented Larry with a silver cup and a lifetime admission pass. But his biggest surprise came on a qualification day in 1967. Over the track's public address system, I called for him to report to the starting line. There, a group of Indianapolis businessmen presented Larry with an elegant new Ford van, equipped for camping. As of 1986, the odometer showed well over 200,000 miles.

But Larry didn't use his van for the '86 race—in fact, it looked as though he wasn't coming. When Larry failed to appear at the front of the line on schedule, local news reporters began a search only to learn that his health was not good enough to permit the exhausting drive. Offers to assist poured into *The Indianapolis Star* and Larry eventually flew to the race as guest of the area's Ford Dealers. Larry trusts this was simply an off year and that he will return on time next year. He will celebrate his ninetieth birthday in 1988.

There are thousands of Speedway fans who envy Larry's "pole position." They begin arriving on the Friday before Sunday's race. Like Larry, many will live in their vehicles until the race is concluded. A nonstop celebration quickly blooms in the areas around the track. Cars loaded with fans, food and drink park near the oval, where they party until race-day morning. Sleep is impossible. Hulman Boulevard becomes a twenty-four-hour carnival for three long days and nights. Temporary food and souvenir stands line the streets. Throngs of fans wander aimlessly, clogging Georgetown Road on the west side of the track. A forty-acre parking lot on the track's north end is jammed with campers and autos.

These spectators will pay ten dollars each for admission to the infield. Some enter with the hope of getting close enough to actually watch the race. Others don't seem to care whether they can see the action or not; they come to join the festivities.

The most convenient sleeping quarters are at the Speedway Motel, on Hulman Boulevard just outside Turn Two. However, a comfortable bed and privacy don't guarantee sleep. Just across from the motel is a large campground inhabited by masses of party-minded celebrants. If the explosion of fireworks doesn't keep you up, then the amplified rock music, piercing yells, and police and ambulance sirens will surely do the job. Some guests—such as drivers A. J. Foyt, Mario Andretti and Danny Ongais— seem to be impervious to the noise and hoopla. Magically, they always look well rested on the day of the race.

Start Your Engines

If you've ever driven the Los Angeles freeways or the streets of Manhattan during rush hour, you'll be prepared for the long wait to enter the Speedway's 559-acre grounds. When the gates swing open at six a.m. on race day, fifteen lines of bumper-to-bumper traffic enter the grounds, while two other entrances are reserved for pedestrians.

An estimated 120,000 people avoid the traffic by taking Indianapolis city buses or calling Dick Hunt's Yellow Cab Company. The buses and taxis sweep riders from downtown into the Speedway in just eight minutes along a special bus and taxi route prohibited to private vehicles. This public transit works fine in the hours before the race, but when those same 120,000 fans try to depart simultaneously after the race, the system breaks down. Some clubs and businesses rent tour buses. Space for 150 buses is reserved outside of Turn Four and another 300 can be parked on Hulman Boulevard just across from the main gate.

For many spectators, arriving on the infield several hours before starting time means another opportunity to party. And if some of the youthful crowd get too rowdy, there's a portable jail outside of Turn Two. Those arrested have to wait inside the hot "jail" bus until it's full, then they're driven to the county jail.

With the bulk of the crowd inside the Speedway, weather reports become headline news. Workers and spectators pray for clear skies, knowing that if the race is rained out, the whole process has to be repeated the next day, and even up to a week later, as happened in 1986.

Room and a View

For years I was amazed by infield spectators who arrived with truckloads of scaffolding. Quickly bolting together platform frames, these enterprising fans would sell seats in the makeshift structures. The most ambitious built stands soaring forty feet into the air. Jammed to the limit with rambunctious fans, it was inevitable that eventually one of these stands would collapse. One did in 1960. Two people were killed and twenty-two injured when a tower fell during the race. After that tragedy, Speedway officials banned the construction of temporary structures in the infield.

The best view of the action can be had from one of the 250,000 reserved seats or one of the hospitality suites. These seats are sold out months before the race. A select group of fans buys the same seats year after year, and they can keep them as long as their renewal requests are mailed in time. Ticket order forms are printed in the Speedway souvenir program: The wise postmark their orders the day after the race.

The most expensive seats are found in the Paddock

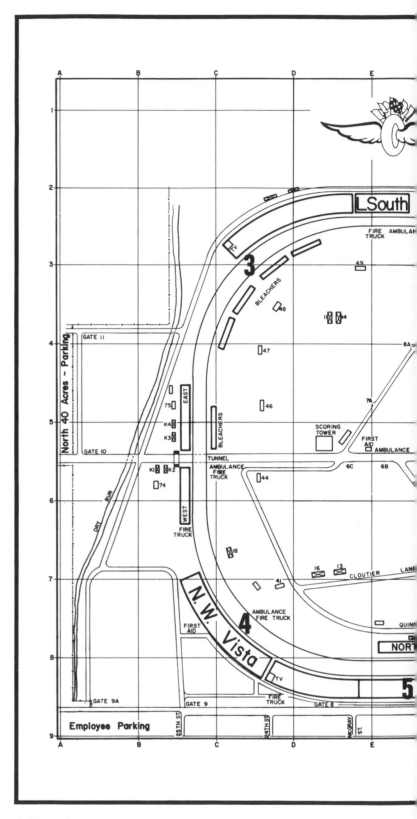

1 Turn One   **2 Turn Two**

INDIANAPOLIS MOTOR SPEEDWAY, INC.

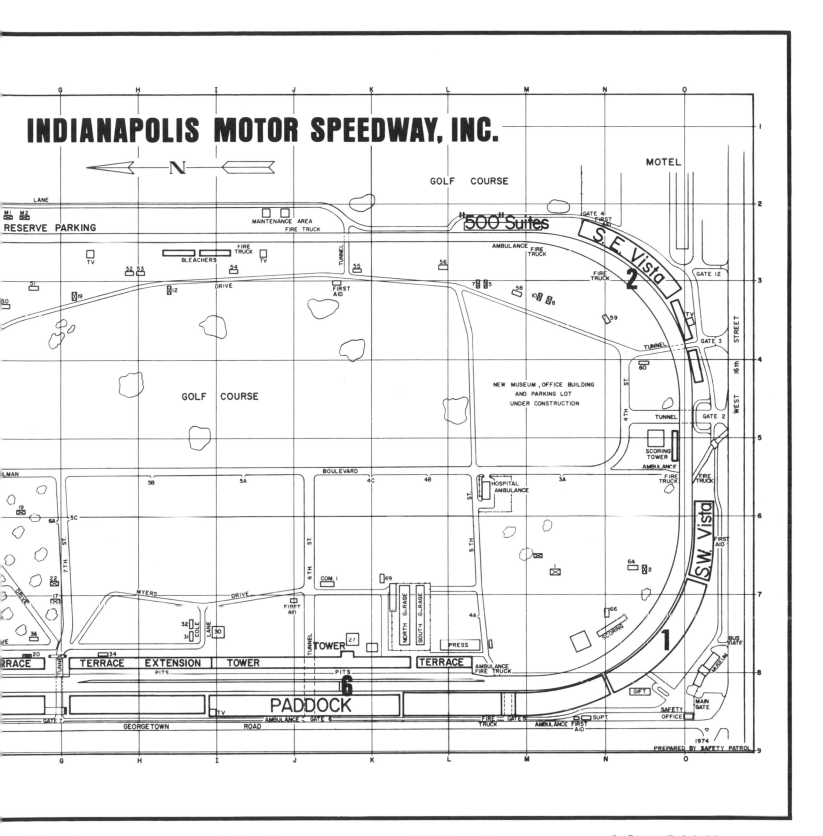

3 Turn Three **4 Turn Four** **5 Hulman Terrace** **6 Start-finish Line**

Mom Unser's Indy Chili
(4 to 6 servings)
1 pound lean pork or beef
1 medium onion, chopped
1 clove garlic, chopped
Oil
1 can (20 ounces) tomatoes
3 small cans mild or medium-hot green chilies
Dash oregano
Salt to taste

Remove all fat from meat. Cube meat. Sauté meat cubes, onion and garlic in a little oil. Mash tomatoes; add with juice to meat mixture. Add chilies, oregano and salt. Simmer about 35 minutes until done, adding more water if necessary. Pinto beans may be added if desired.

Arizona Mountain Bean Soup
(10 to 12 servings)
1 pound pinto beans
1 pound bacon, diced
1 cup uncooked rice
4 cups chopped onions
1½ pounds lean ham, cubed
3 large tomatoes
2 tablespoons minced garlic
2 teaspoons paprika
2 teaspoons garlic salt
Salt and pepper to taste

Cook pinto beans according to package directions. Cook rice in 2 cups water. Fry diced bacon until crisp, drain on paper towels. Reserve ½ cup bacon drippings to sauté chopped onions. Peel and dice tomatoes.

Mix cooked pinto beans, including the liquid, with cooked bacon and onions. Add rice, ham cubes, tomatoes, and garlic, paprika, garlic salt, salt and pepper in large kettle. Bring to low simmer and simmer for 2 hours, stirring occasionally. If soup thickens, add a little water while cooking.

Penthouse, atop a grandstand directly across from the starting line, and the Stand A Penthouse box seats, located along the main stretch from south of the starting line extending into Turn One. The seats tower high above the ground, affording a panoramic view of the track and pits. Seats here sell for eighty dollars each. Reserved grandstand seats across from the pits and extending into the first turn are forty-five dollars. Seats behind the pits are forty-five dollars, while those in other locations sell for fifteen, twenty and twenty-five dollars.

The hospitality suites are the ultimate race-day location. And although the price is steep, averaging $30,000 annually, most lease-holders think the investment worthwhile. The high price hardly affects sales; there's a long waiting list of at least a hundred names, including companies as well as individuals. Most of them will wait years before they get the chance to bid on a suite. Thirty suites, called the 500 Suites, were built outside of Turn Two in 1973; twenty-seven additional suites, known as the Hulman Terrace, were added along the north end of the main straightaway in 1984. Each suite includes a section of eighty penthouse seats with excellent views of the track. But if a fan prefers to eat and drink inside, closed-circuit television provides a live view of all the action.

Memory Lane

When the race starts, I begin describing the drama as it unfolds. As the official Speedway announcer, I've called every race since 1946. It's an intense but relatively easy job—all I need are the words. I've been primed by my experiences during the month of practice, through qualifying week, and endless parties, fashion shows, press meetings, dinners and speeches. For me, the tough part is over. Reporting the race is easy.

Likewise, a veteran Indy-goer will arrive early in the month of May, absorb the tradition, learn the history, study the pre-trial contenders and enjoy the social events along the way.

More than a million visitors start their initiation to

Indy at the Hall of Fame each year. This museum, housing one of the world's finest automotive collections, features over two hundred vintage autos and more than twenty-five cars that have won the Indy 500. Here is the Indy story at a glance, from Harroun's 1911 Marmon Wasp to Rutherford's 1980 Chaparral Racing Limited.

The museum reflects the passionate devotion of its late owner Tony Hulman. No one could compete with his enthusiasm for collecting historical models, as I found out in the 1960s when my employer, Eldon Campbell, sent me to an auction in quest of a certain Model A Ford. With a blank check in hand, I waited for the auction to start. Suddenly, Tony Hulman appeared; he had his eyes on the same Model A. When the bidding was over, Hulman had added another fine trophy to his already impressive collection and I returned to Indianapolis with Campbell's check still in my wallet.

Spring Rituals

The Speedway officially opens on the first Saturday in May, three weeks and one day before the race. The public is invited to a breakfast in downtown Indianapolis hosted by the mayor, then it's on to the track for the opening ceremonies. Joe Cloutier, Speedway President, turns the track over to the United States Auto Club (USAC) officials. When the green light comes on for the first practice, several drivers vie for the honor (not to mention free publicity) of taking the first lap.

From then on there's plenty of roadwork and testing at the track to prepare for the qualification trials, held the second and third weekends before the race. Many drivers and fans alike look upon the qualification trials as the most fascinating race event of all—a competition against time and unpredictable odds to become one of thirty-three drivers to make the starting field. As many as 200,000 spectators attend the first day of qualifying.

In the late 60s and early 70s, safety director Joe Quinn wanted to capitalize on this ready-made audience. A genius for promotion, Joe decided to follow historical precedent: The very first race held at the Speedway in 1909 was not an auto race, but a hot-air balloon race launched to attract crowds to the new track.

Taking his cue from that race, Joe staged balloon ascensions on the third day of qualifying. Most years, the show was a big crowd-pleaser. Sometime in the mid-1970s, things went a bit awry. The weather was marginal, but Joe gave the go-ahead anyway. A powerful crosswind caught one of the balloonists when he was just a few feet off the ground, spinning the giant craft across the infield at top speed. Man and balloon hit a women's toilet full tilt, turning it completely over and severely startling the two occupants. That was the end of balloon ascensions at the Speedway, but not the end of the incident. The two ladies sued; the Speedway later spent about a million dollars to rebuild all of its toilet facilities, and these are now quite properly balloon-proof.

Celebrate Good Times

In between practice and qualifying, there are three solid weeks of special events and parties. Perhaps the most famous of these were the annual chili parties hosted by Mom Unser near Gasoline Alley. Although the gatherings drew drivers, officials and fans, with the exception of her sons Bobby and Al, few were able to handle the fiery concoction without discomfort—the chili peppers were said to be the most potent in New Mexico. When Mom died in 1975, the chili parties ended, but her recipe is a Speedway legacy.

These days the racing fraternity has become addicted to Betty Dunham's "Arizona Bean Soup." After the first weekend of qualifications, Phil and Betty Dunham host a rookie party at their home. Even though the neophyte drivers honored at the fête eventually shed their "rookie stripes," they return year after year for Betty's western-style feast, and the Press Room always requests gallons of soup for Carburetion Day.

After racing, eating becomes a major social activity

for the month of May at Indy. In 1983 the Indiana National Bank began sponsoring the Leaders' Circle Banquet, an informal affair held annually on the Speedway grounds honoring drivers who have led one or more laps in an Indy 500 race.

Another dinner, held in town at the Indianapolis Athletic Club, bestows the Jim Clark Award—an honor given to the driver or race official who exemplifies the qualities of the Indianapolis winner and former World Champion Jim Clark.

Rich food and rich accommodations are only part of the Indianapolis story. The record books hint at the vibrant tradition that has contributed so much to the success of the Speedway. At the annual 500 Oldtimers Barbeque, drivers, car owners, chief mechanics and officials—whose contributions defy mere statistical compilation—bring flesh-and-blood meaning to the numbers. Each year since the mid-1950s, the Oldtimers gather on the Monday after qualifications. Here you can meet driver Ira Hall, who first competed at Indianapolis in 1928, or you can hear Duke Nalon's harrowing description of how he survived the fiery Novi crash of 1949.

Practice, Practice, Practice

Thursday before the race Indy really gets moving. About 75,000 people are on hand to watch three events: final pit practice, final testing of the thirty-three qualified cars, and the Miller Pit Stop Contest. Traditionally this activity was called Carburetion Day, but that's a misnomer. Fuel-injection systems replaced carburetors on the race cars many decades ago.

Early in the day, teams run through their pit stop procedures. Five mechanics do the work—two men fuel the car while three others change the tires. One takes care of the front tires and makes wing adjustments while the other two change the rear tires and push the car out of the pit. The fueler handling the vent hose also works the air hose. When a machine stops in the pit, he connects the air hose to a special coupling that feeds a pneumatic jack built into the car. The jack automatically raises

the car so the tires can be changed. When the tires are secured, the hose is disconnected and the car drops to the ground.

The final practice runs before race day come next. The engine that will power the car during the race has been installed, and it's the last check to make sure it's ready. The crews check for oil, fuel or hydraulic fluid leaks and make their final calculations of miles per gallon.

Two or three sets of tires are "scuffed in": As each new set is put on, the driver takes a couple of fast laps to heat up the tires; then the tires are taken off and, once they cool down, the diameter of each tire is carefully measured. The purpose is to have each set of replacement tires with the same diameter and "stagger" as the set that was used during the qualifying laps. Even minute differences in the diameter of a tire affect the car's handling, particularly at the high speeds run at Indianapolis. The tires that are on the car when it qualifies *must* be used to start the race. When a car qualifies, USAC officials impound the tires immediately, and they aren't returned until race day.

Pit Bulls

Once the track testing is complete, fans are treated to the annual Miller Pit Stop Contest. Begun in 1977, it's a frenzy of excitement fueled by cash prizes in excess of $50,000. For the first nine years, eight teams competed in the finals: The four fastest qualifiers from the starting field of thirty-three were automatically eligible, and the other four were selected based on their pit stop times during qualifying competition. Starting in 1986, the field was trimmed to just four teams.

Two mock pit walls are placed side by side in the pit lane so that two cars can make pit stops at the same time. At the green flag, the competing machines are driven into the pits, two teams at a time. For the first run-offs, the waiting crews change both right side wheels, and when the car is dropped to the ground and pushed away, the stop is complete. Penalties of five to ten seconds are imposed for

irregularities, such as running over air hoses, or if the crew members leap over the wall too soon or fail to tighten lug nuts or lay the wheels flat. The two teams with the fastest stops then compete in the finals. Until the '86 race, the finalists were timed for a two-tire pitstop, including a simulated refueling. New rules added a four-tire change.

The record pit stop was 11.472 seconds, set in 1985 by Danny Sullivan's crew. When the record was set, Howdy Holmes's crew was actually eight-thousandths of a second faster than Sullivan's, but a ten-second penalty was assessed for an air-hose violation. That tiny slip cost the team $10,000. Sullivan's crew won the $20,000 first prize, while the Holmes team came away with $10,000 for their second-place finish. It was an expensive lesson in being fast and efficient in the pit. Being fast and efficient in the pit is even more important on race day. The same year that Sullivan's crew set the pit stop record, Sullivan won the race.

Sullivan stopped eight times during the race: twice for fuel only and six times for both fuel and tires. On the fourth stop, the crew changed three tires and fueled the car in just thirteen seconds. Sullivan's total time in the pit was just 121 seconds, an average of 15 seconds per stop!

Thursday ends with a Pole Position Mechanics Banquet in the Speedway infield. All thirty-three crew chiefs are saluted, while the chief of the team that took the pole position receives cash and other bonuses.

Dance Fever

Friday begins with a parade of a different sort: Drivers and their wives model the latest fashions during a luncheon at the Indianapolis Convention Center. It's all for a good cause, as the money raised goes to charities aided by the Championship Auto Racing Auxiliary.

A relatively new Friday feature is the Mini-Marathon. Seven thousand runners depart from Monument Circle on a thirteen-mile course that ends at the Speedway's finish line. The social season

climaxes with the Queen's Ball on Friday night. The gala honors the Queen of the 500 Festival, chosen from among thirty-three princesses representing various Indiana colleges and universities.

One to Get Ready

At eleven a.m. on Saturday, the drivers are outwardly jovial. They smile, greet friends enthusiastically and chat amiably with fellow competitors. As I introduce them, the crowd responds with cheers, yet I wonder how the drivers feel? Their faces are calm, with no sign of concern. This is the annual drivers' meeting, and the public is invited.

The green flag that starts the 500 drops exactly twenty-four hours later. The race stewards and track officials give the drivers final instructions and their best wishes. The drivers ask a few procedural questions, a half-dozen special awards are presented, and the ceremony ends. Fans love this part of the program, when they can really see the drivers. On race day, the drivers will be hunkered down in the cockpits of their racing machines. All that remain visible are the gaily-colored helmets. But on Saturday the drivers appear in street clothes, in full view, smiling confidently.

The drivers are then escorted downtown for the start of the 500 Festival Parade, an annual feature since 1957, and now televised nationally. An estimated 300,000 spectators line the streets to greet the champions, admire the floats and follow the bands. Although entertainers and other celebrities are part of the festivities, all eyes are on the drivers. The gaiety continues late into the night at hundreds of pre-race parties. The wise send their regrets in favor of a good night's sleep.

Victory

The ultimate party—Victory Dinner—is held in the Hoosier Dome for a crowd of 2,000. Every driver who attends the dinner is a winner, but there can only be one champion. That driver deserves the congratulations, respect and sincere admiration that

come with victory. He also takes home the lion's share of the cash prize. While the exact dollar figure is never known until just prior to the introduction of the drivers, the purse has mushroomed over the years. From $96,000 in the early 1940s, it's grown to over four million dollars.

As the dinner winds down, the words of the late Tony Hulman come back: "We hope you fully enjoy America's greatest sporting event." Exhausted but exhilarated, Indianapolis can't wait to have another go at it!

Dawn. The sun peers over the rim of the world in search of a new day. At this early hour, the great grandstands of the Indianapolis Motor Speedway are only a low, flat line across the horizon. They stand silent, waiting.

Within hours, they will sag beneath the weight of the largest single sporting event on the face of the earth. More than 235,000 fans in reserved seats. Another 100,000-plus lining the fences, packing the infield.

The city of Indianapolis prepares all year for this, its most glorious hour. During the month of May, enormous crowds gather at the track on qualification days, then it's parades, balls, parties and more parties. On race day, marching bands and majorettes strut down pit lane, while movie stars and celebrities bask in the borrowed glamour of this vast celebration of speed and bravery.

All the while, deep within the Indianapolis Motor Speedway Garage Area, a desperate battle is raging. Behind closed doors, the racing teams work feverishly to complete the last crucial tasks—tasks that could mean the difference between great speed and quiet mediocrity, between triumph and defeat, between life and death.

Wheels and suspension pieces are magnafluxed to uncover hidden metallurgic flaws that might cause them to disintegrate under the strain of cornering at 200-plus mph. Engines and gearboxes are assembled, installed, checked, re-checked. Multiple sets of racing tires are mounted on wheels for use during the many pit stops. Troublesome cockpit radio systems are tested, and tested again. Team-strategy meetings are held in strict secrecy behind locked doors. To the vast crowd in the grandstands, the Indy 500 is a joyous festival. To the racers, it is a war.

On race-day morning when the great checkered canopy (overleaf) releases its tens of thousands of multicolored balloons for the 11 a.m. start, the crowd will cheer and whoop—let the festival begin!

For the racing teams, it signals but one thing—the struggle is under way.

Godspeed.

Racing's First Family

ate in the 1985 season, on a temporary road race course in Miami, unfolded one of the most remarkable competitive dramas ever to be played out in any sport. A cagey veteran driver and a twenty-three-year-old youngster were set to do battle in the final race of the year, ending a fierce campaign for the CART National Championship.

The older man, broad-shouldered, with crow's feet just starting to appear around eyes set in what has long been described as a baby face, was characteristically quiet, thoughtful and focused. The younger of the two, fresh-faced and freckled, displayed a small-town deference toward everyone more than five years older, whom he invariably addressed as "sir." But his eyes sparkled with a sharp, undisguised ambition: to be the best, and to prove it by winning the championship title.

Just three points separated the two men in the standings. This day, on the blistering-hot asphalt of suburban Miami, they would prove who was the better driver. The race was remarkable, not only for the intensity of the rivalry and the narrowness of the margin between them, but because the two men about to determine the 1985 National Championship were father and son: Al Unser Sr. and Al Unser Jr.

Al Sr., forty-five years old and already the owner of two national championships, was driving for Penske Racing. He had won the previous race in Phoenix, Arizona, his only first-place finish of the year, to build the slim, three-point lead over his son, who was driving for Team Shierson. Mario Andretti, the 1984 champion, Bobby Rahal and Emerson Fittipaldi had been in the title chase all season. The championship point system (twenty points for first place, sixteen for second, fourteen for third . . . through one point for twelfth) rewards consistency,

so by the end of the year, the Unsers had pulled ahead of these challengers. Now the battle was a clash between father and son.

It was remarkable that the father was even in a position to contend for the title. At the start of the season, team owner Roger Penske had guaranteed him rides only in the three 500-mile events—Indianapolis, Michigan and Pocono—on the fifteen-race schedule. However, the team's number-one driver, Speedway champion Rick Mears, was still recovering from severe leg injuries suffered the previous season. Rick did drive at Indianapolis and then at another oval-course race in Milwaukee. But, with his legs still not completely healed, Mears decided to forgo road racing, which requires continuous braking and shifting. His legs simply weren't ready. Penske moved Al into competition full time. To the credit of Rick Mears, he led the Al Unser cheering section, serving as test driver, helping set up the machine for Al at race after race. It was as if the likeable Mears were campaigning the machine himself.

Meanwhile, Al Jr. had captured two races, at Cleveland and New Jersey's Meadowlands, and had finished high enough in the others on the CART circuit to lead the point battle—until, that is, his dad assumed command at the Phoenix race. At mid-season Al Jr. crashed and broke an ankle in the race at Elkhart Lake, Wisconsin. After being flown to Methodist Hospital in Indianapolis for repairs, he unbelievably raced two weeks later in the 500-miler at Pocono International Raceway in Long Pond, Pennsylvania. So when the race in Miami started, the nation knew that an Unser would win the driving title, but which one?

Neither Unser contended for the lead that day. But with Penske's other driver, Danny Sullivan, having won the race going into the final few laps, the battle between the Unsers became the center of interest. Al Unser Jr. led his dad throughout the race, but then Al Sr. found a way around Roberto Moreno to move just one position behind his son.

That's the way they finished—Jr. in third and Sr. in

fourth. But the fourth-place finish gave Al Sr. enough points to win the title, edging out his son by the margin of a single point! Fittingly, the expert commentator describing the action for NBC television was Al's brother, Bobby. Between them, Al and Bobby had won six Indianapolis 500s by 1985. And now once again it was sure enough an Unser day!

When the checkered flag dropped and Al Sr. had won the championship, the younger Unser drew up alongside his father. Al Jr.'s gloved hand briefly left the steering wheel to render an affectionate salute. And with that small wave, he showed both his true feelings for his dad and the quality of his own sportsmanship. After this classic finish, Al Jr. commented: "My dad taught me all I know about racing, but he hasn't taught me all *he* knows."

And so the National Championship trophy again resides in Albuquerque, New Mexico. The Unsers are part of the rugged and beautiful land of New Mexico; it has always been their home and probably always will be. Had Bobby and Al lived in the area a century earlier, I'm certain they would have been gunfighters. Wearing a lawman's badge, the fearless pair would have swept the territory clean of desperadoes. Unser Boulevard, a major exit off Interstate 40, is today a tribute to the affection New Mexicans have for this famous clan.

Born to Run

The Unser family story begins in Colorado Springs, Colorado. In the Depression years of the early 1930s, Jerry Unser—"Daddy," as the sons still refer to him—owned a garage there. Daddy also drove in the annual Pike's Peak race. That event, to the top of the 14,110-foot peak, is truly owned by the Unsers. Bobby has captured the climb eleven times, Al twice, and their uncle, Louis Unser, won it nine times. Jerry met his wife, the former Mary Craven, in Colorado Springs in 1931. Their courtship lasted only two weeks, and they were married when Daddy was thirty-one and Mary, "Mom" to the Unser clan, was twenty-four.

In 1933 the first of the Unsers' four sons were born, twins Jerry Jr. and Louis. Bobby was born a year later, and Al arrived in 1939. With a growing family and a garage that couldn't support them, the Unsers opened a restaurant. It proved a mistake. Even though it took years, the family paid back every debt that resulted from that failure.

Without a job, Daddy took the bus to Albuquerque, where a real-estate boom was underway. He was determined to return to the auto business and picked a spot just outside town on Highway 66. His was the first garage for motorists arriving from the west after crossing the 325 miles of high desert that separate Albuquerque from Flagstaff, Arizona. Eventually, Daddy purchased 300 acres of land on both sides of this highway.

Bobby and Al still live on Daddy's land: Bobby and his wife, Marsha, on the south side of the highway, Al and Karen across the road. Despite their national acclaim and financial success, they choose to live on the family property, disdaining the life of luxury they might have elsewhere. Perhaps battling the elements has honed their skills, making them more competitive on the racetrack. Al Jr. and his wife Shelley live just a few miles away on the banks of the Rio Grande.

It was natural that the Unser boys would be exposed to automobiles. The few racetracks around Albuquerque soon became their center of interest. But who would believe that such beginnings would lead to an all-out assault on Indianapolis by the sons!

Starting Line

The beginning of the Indianapolis success story, however, was a tragic one. It was Jerry Jr. as driver and Louis as chief mechanic who, at the age of twenty-five, arrived at Indianapolis in May 1958. Jerry was big, standing just over six feet and weighing 220 pounds; high-school football and wrestling were in his background prior to becoming a stock-car racer. Jerry appeared at Indy with a De Soto-powered roadster that was several years old. Though the car showed no promise of qualifying,

Louis's skilled work on the engine held the brute together long enough for Jerry to pass his driver's test. But there was no hope of getting it up to the speeds needed to make the starting field.

Then in the final week of practice, driver Don Edmunds called Jerry and Louis to his garage. Don had crashed earlier in the month, and the car had been rebuilt. But after a couple of near-accidents caused by a sticky throttle, Edmunds had had enough, and offered the ride to his friend, Jerry. The Unser team got the machine qualified on the final day and wound up in twenty-fourth position on the starting grid, on the outside of the eighth row.

On the very first lap of the race, the two leading cars—Dick Rathmann and Ed Elisian—tangled in the third turn. Before the wild melee was over, fifteen cars were knocked out of competition. Pat O'Connor was killed, and Jerry Unser's car climbed over Paul Goldsmith's roadster and then catapulted over the wall and out of the track. When Jerry was pulled from the shattered machine, he complained of nothing more than a sore shoulder. At the track hospital, medics popped the dislocated shoulder back into place, and Jerry started making plans for the next season. That's the spirit of the incredible Unsers!

Jerry returned to Indianapolis the next year. He was out early on the second day of practice, May 2, 1959. Though not traveling at high speeds, somehow his car went out of control and hit both the inside and outside walls in Turn Four. The machine caught fire, and Jerry, pinned in the cockpit, was badly burned before the flames could be extinguished. For a time it seemed as if Jerry was improving, but two weeks after the accident, he died, not from burns, but from blood poisoning.

A distraught Louis Unser jumped from one activity to another after his twin brother's death. He accepted a challenge to join a Mercury stock team that was to race from Cape Horn, Africa, to Fairbanks, Alaska, in forty-four days. The race went off as planned, but prior to the start, Louis learned that he had multiple sclerosis. Now confined to a wheelchair, Louis lives in California, where he's a marine-engine mechanic.

Bobby Hits the Brickyard

Four years after Jerry Jr.'s fatal accident, brother Bobby was the next Unser to try Indianapolis. It was 1963, and Bobby was twenty-nine years old. The tall, lean, wiry young man with the roguish smile had raced sprint cars, but he'd never competed at the high speeds run at Indianapolis. Still, Bobby Unser had an intense determination to succeed.

Bobby's practice runs at the Speedway in an antiquated Offenhauser roadster brought a 1,000-foot slide and a stop at the wall. It was clear that the tired machine was simply not good enough to make the field. Then veteran driver Parnelli Jones talked to Andy Granatelli, a legendary impresario of the Speedway and manufacturer of STP oil. Jones recommended that Granatelli give Bobby a chance to drive the Novi. With over 820 horsepower, Bobby quickly hit nearly 150 mph. The seat in one of the three Novis belonged to Bobby. The other two drivers were Jim Hurtubise and Art Malone. The second weekend of qualifying found Bobby making the show at 149.421 mph, landing him a sixth-row starting position in the field of thirty-three.

But Bobby would race only briefly that Memorial Day. On the second lap, underestimating his speed on a corner, Bobby got the Novi sideways and then piled into the wall backwards. It was a terrific crash, and although the fuel tank ruptured, there was no fire and Bobby wasn't hurt. It was not a particularly successful debut.

Often a rookie driver who crashes in his first start at the 500 looks in vain for a ride the following year. But Granatelli obviously felt Bobby showed promise, and Unser once again found himself in the ill-fated Novi in 1964. That year Granatelli unveiled the unconventional four-wheel drive system. After endless laps of practice, Bobby's speeds again reached nearly 150 mph. Then the Novi's engine blew, and Unser went through a 600-foot slide but

Al, Louie, Daddy, Bobby and Jerry Jr.

To my Mother
with Love, Louis

LOOP CAFE
SPECIAL

14

Daddy's brother Louis

Joe

Daddy's brother Joe

Jerry, Al, Daddy, Louie and Bobby

Jerry, Al, Louie and Bobby

Al Sr.

Bobby Jr.

Bobby, Mom, Daddy and Al "WINNER"

Louie, Bobby, Mom and Al

Bobby, Daddy and Al

stayed away from the outer wall. A few days later, another engine exploded. This time, the result was an 800-foot slide, again avoiding the wall. Then, during the first weekend of qualifying, another engine blew, so Unser had to wait until the second weekend. His mark, 154.865 mph, was fifth quickest in the field. But by not qualifying until the final weekend, he was forced to start well back in the eighth row.

Tragedy struck early in the 1964 race. Eddie Sachs and Dave MacDonald were killed in a second-lap pileup at the head of the main stretch. Unser, along with Ronnie Duman and Johnny Rutherford, was caught up in the accident. Bobby suffered only second-degree burns on his neck.

In two years of racing, Bobby Unser had totaled just three laps of actual competition. But Granatelli still believed in him. The next year, 1965, Bobby crashed into Ebb Rose during practice but made the field and ran some 200 miles before an oil leak ended his third effort.

Tired of the Novi jinx, Bobby signed to drive a new machine owned by Gordon Van Liew, finishing eighth in the 1966 race. The following year he shifted to the Leader Card team out of Milwaukee and came in ninth. Staying with the Leader Card team in 1968, Bobby qualified with the third fastest time. Joe Leonard, a two-time USAC champion, led the classic in a Granatelli turbine, but it expired just nine laps from the finish. Unser moved into first place, captured his first Indianapolis victory, and set a new record average speed for the run, 152 mph. While some might say that Bobby won because Leonard's turbine failed, Unser did lead 127 of the 200 laps. Bobby went on to win the USAC National Championship in a stirring duel with Mario Andretti.

Al's Fast Start

Three years before, in 1965, Bobby's younger brother Al had made a successful debut at Indianapolis. With a junkyard and a family to take care of, Al had done most of his racing around Albuquerque. Despite a lack of experience, Al teamed up with his older brother Louis—again the chief mechanic—to prepare a Maserati-powered machine owned by Frank Arciero of California. It did not have enough power to make the field, but in the final two hours of qualifications on the fourth day, Al was given a ride in A.J. Foyt's new Lola. He qualified and then raced, finishing ninth for Foyt. It was the first time two Unsers, Bobby and Al, were in the starting field.

Driving as a teammate of Jim Clark the next year, Al finished twelfth. He might have finished higher, but he crashed just forty laps from the finish. Then began the first year of a highly productive relationship with chief mechanic George Bignotti. Al finished a stunning second behind A.J. Foyt in 1967, but crashed the next year on the forty-first lap.

Home Court

The only way to truly understand a driver is to visit his home ground, away from the distractions of Indy. With Bobby's win and Al's promise, it was time for me to visit New Mexico. I arrived in Albuquerque with a television crew in the winter of 1968. We would be visiting both sides of Highway 66. The quiet, reserved Al lived on the north side, still operating the junkyard his father had helped him start; Speedway champion Bobby lived on the south side.

But that visit Mom Unser was the real star. Husband Jerry had died in 1967 without seeing an Unser in Victory Lane at Indianapolis. Women were not permitted in either the garage or the pit area at the Speedway in those years, so I knew Mom only by sight. Her healthy Southwestern tan, silver hair and strong hands spoke of her frontier heritage. She greeted me wearing her favorite windbreaker. Because her sons were sponsored by rival tire companies, half of her jacket proclaimed loyalty to Goodyear, while the other half lauded Firestone. Her decal boasted "Fireyear," while her husband Jerry's jacket had tooted the complementary cheer "Goodstone."

Not knowing quite what to expect, I walked into the Unser living room and spotted an organ.

"Who plays that?" I lamely inquired.

"I do," replied Mom. "I have a master's degree in music from Lindenwood College in Missouri."

I must admit that I was shocked—and impressed. Being from Missouri, I told her that I knew Lindenwood College by reputation, and added that I had graduated from William Jewell College, also in Missouri.

"My father attended William Jewell," Mom quietly confided.

We quickly became friends. With Mom's educational background and work experience as a teacher, she expressed keen disappointment that her sons had not graduated from high school, electing to work in their father's garage instead. There was no trace of disappointment, however, when we talked about her boys starting a dynasty of Unser-family winners at Indy.

Racer's Edge

It certainly came as no surprise when the Unsers began to win at Indianapolis. They were raised for this challenge, it seems, and the mechanical skills honed by their father enabled them to communicate with pit crews and aid in setting up a race car. Race victories for Bobby and Al came with expected regularity. With George Bignotti as his crew chief, Al won two straight Indianapolis races in 1970 and again in 1971, setting a new track record in 1971 when he averaged 157.735 mph. Bobby returned to Victory Lane in 1975, driving an Eagle chassis for Dan Gurney. With just twenty-six laps to go, a slashing rainstorm roared through the Speedway, abruptly ending a duel between Bobby and Johnny Rutherford for the finish. Bobby was given the checkered flag as he hydroplaned across the traditional row of bricks at the starting line on Lap 174, at a speed of 149.213. Three years later, Al Unser won his third Indy when he finished just eight seconds ahead of Tom Sneva. Al won this time for car owner Jim Hall, with Hywell (Hughie)

Absalom as chief mechanic. The winner's purse was almost $300,000.

Million-Dollar Challenge

Bobby Unser's third Indianapolis crown came in 1981, but only after a summer of controversy. Unser took the checkered flag in a Norton Spirit owned by Penske Racing, finishing almost six seconds ahead of Mario Andretti, who had moved up from thirty-second position to challenge for the victory. But when the official results were posted at eight a.m. the next morning at the USAC office in Gasoline Alley, they showed Andretti the winner! A one-lap penalty had been assessed against Bobby by chief steward Tom Binford for an alleged violation. It was the first time a driver had been stripped of an Indianapolis victory. Thus began the longest controversy in Speedway history.

The victory dinner that evening was anything but fun. I was the emcee, and it was certainly not an occasion for the usual celebration. Andretti was presented the pace car as part of the traditional victor's prize—but he was not given the keys. The huge winner's prize of $300,000 was announced, but the pay envelope given to Mario was empty. The decision by Binford and the race stewards had been officially appealed by Bobby Unser; prizes could not be awarded until a hearing was held and a ruling made.

USAC board of directors appointed a three-judge panel, and hearings began on June 4. Unser was charged with passing eight cars while under a caution light as he transversed the exit apron on the inside of the track after making a pit stop at the end of the 149th lap. Testimony concluded July 31, with Unser and Andretti the star witnesses. Unser even convinced the judges to accompany him on a tour of the oval so he could present his case firsthand. A NASCAR spokesman was a telling witness, saying that it struck at the very integrity of racing to change winners after a race.

Finally, almost four months after Unser visited Victory Lane, the race was given back to him in a

In January 1986 President Reagan invited the entire Unser family to the Oval Office for special ceremonies honoring racing's most famous family.

split decision by the panel of judges. The one-lap penalty was rescinded and replaced with a $40,000 fine. Bobby Unser, then forty-seven years old, had the race he'd "won" 138 days before, $300,000, and the keys to the pace car. The following winter, Bobby stunned the racing fraternity by announcing that his driving career was over. "It was just time," he said. And though he harbored no bitterness over the previous summer's dispute, he did later confide to me that he figured the delay in his certification as the 1981 Indy winner cost him almost a million dollars in endorsements.

Father and Son Reunion

Two years later, in 1983, the Indianapolis 500 boasted a father-and-son combination for the first time. Al Unser Jr., one of six rookies in the field, was entered by Rick Galles of Albuquerque, a longtime friend of the Unsers. Schooled by his father, Al Jr. was now provided with first-rate equipment by Galles.

The race itself was fun to watch. Here were Al Unser Sr. and Tom Sneva running one-two right at the end of the 500 miles. Tucked in between Al and Tom was Little Al, who by his driving seemed to be making it tough for Tom to pass him and go to work on Al Sr.'s lead. Al Jr. ran out of fuel eight laps from the finish, and Sneva went on to pass Al Sr. and win his first 500.

President Ronald Reagan officially recognized the contribution of the Unsers in January 1986. He invited the entire Unser family to the Oval Office for special ceremonies honoring racing's most famous family. The White House guest list included Marsha and Bobby Unser, Karen and Al Unser, Shelley and Al Unser Jr., and their son, Al Richard. So now it's Big Al, Little Al, and Mini Al. Hopefully the Unser era will never end!

What does any parent think, knowing that his son has chosen to pursue one of the most dangerous professions in human society? Jerry "Daddy" Unser of the racing Unsers (right) was better placed than most fathers to understand the choice made by his sons Bobby and Al. In his younger days, Daddy Unser was a racer too, and so were his two brothers, although neither he nor his brothers ever reached the Indy 500. Racing was in the Unser blood.

It came as no surprise, therefore, when in 1958 eldest son Jerry Unser Jr. made it to Indy. Tragically, the worst happened—in practice for his second 500 in 1959, Jerry Unser Jr. was killed.

Yet racing breeds eternal optimism. Four years later, Daddy Unser's middle son, Bobby, went to Indy. And two years later, young Al Unser—in those days, they called him "Baby Al"—followed brother Bobby to the Speedway.

And Daddy Unser went along to watch. But having two sons competing against each other, his family loyalties were sorely tested. Making matters worse, in the late 1960s Al had a tire contract with Firestone, while Bobby made his contract with Goodyear. Daddy Unser's good-natured attempt to straddle this fence resulted in his famous "Goodstone" jacket.

Daddy and Mom Unser, both beloved fixtures at the Speedway, are gone now, yet the family problem of impartiality continues as before. Although Bobby has retired from Indy cars, Al Unser Jr. has established himself as a major talent, fully capable of competing with his dad for the affection of the Unsers—and the nation.

In 1985 the CART National Championship came down to a last-race duel between the two Als, father and son. Fittingly, the father won over the son, but only by the slimmest of margins.

For most drivers, the finish of the Indy 500 is a moment of grinding defeat, but for Bobby Unser, its joy is boundless. He celebrated that joy in 1968, 1975, and most recently (right, getting the victor's kiss from wife Marsha in Victory Lane) in 1981.

Victory at Indy is sweet—so sweet that it makes up for years of frustration.

Bobby was perhaps the fiercest competitor of his time. Lean, determined, boiling over with aggressive energy, he always got the most out of his cars.

By contrast, brother Al Sr., with his scowling "race face" in place (overleaf), was an elegant strategist, the consummate judge of his car's endurance.

However, while Bobby always pressed his car to go absolutely as fast as it would go, Al typically chose to do his fast running at the end of a race, when it would do the most good. Like Bobby, he too has three Indy wins, in 1970, 1971 and 1978.

In the paralyzing tension immediately before a qualifying attempt (left), Al Jr. walks to his car, while Al Sr., separated from his son by the white cordon of the qualification line, shares his hard-won wisdom.

Successfully qualified (below), Al Jr. smiles in Gasoline Alley, 1985. Despite his evident youth, he has spent a lifetime in racing, beginning with go-karts at age nine, graduating to dangerous dirt-track sprint cars at sixteen. An Indy-car veteran at twenty-three, he is already one of the reigning stars of the circuit.

"Mini Al," the littlest Al of all (above) has yet to win his first race. But is that the glimmer of a Victory Lane smile. . . .

Joe Dawson, Winner 1912

The Most Exciting Races

High drama. That's what makes any sporting event memorable. Not every Indy 500 is packed with the kind of action that typifies car racing at its best, but the odds are good that three years out of five will provide thrills to be remembered for a lifetime.

At Indy, high drama takes a number of forms—the debut of an innovative machine, the setting of new speed records, bizarre turns of events, and wild wheel-to-wheel finishes. Since 1946, I've called every race at the Speedway. While each has supplied a few unforgettable moments, for sheer excitement I'd place my bet that at least six will go down in history.

1912: A "Push" for the Finish

Although Ray Harroun secured his place in the record books by driving a Marmon to victory in the first race at Indianapolis in 1911, it was the colorful Ralph DePalma who the very next year furnished the first spellbinding finish. Fans had paid twenty-five cents to watch twenty-four drivers qualify on the Monday before Memorial Day, 1912. Back then, drivers had to average 75 mph for one full lap before they were permitted to race.

During the race, DePalma, driving a Mercedes, led Joe Dawson by a full five laps with a hundred miles to go. As DePalma finished his 190th lap, fans headed for the exits. Suddenly, his engine began to chatter and spurt oil. The big Mercedes had been struck ill, and it was clearly dying. With each lap, DePalma's machine lost more power. His speed dropped to 60 mph, then 50, then 40. Dawson, driving a National, was still three laps behind. DePalma had only two laps to go. As DePalma entered Turn Four of his second-to-last lap, the engine died. DePalma and his riding mechanic climbed out and began pushing the disabled Mercedes toward the finish line. Dawson roared past them to victory.

The fans reserved their ovation for DePalma, and he returned their cheers with an enthusiastic wave and a smile that belied his true disappointment. Ralph Mulford, the tenth-place finisher that day, completed the 500 in eight hours and fifty-three minutes. He received $1,200 for his efforts. DePalma, who was just two laps from victory, was awarded eleventh place, a "Did not finish" in the record books, and just under $400 in prize money. Three years later, however, DePalma won the championship and later became an auto racing legend.

1946: Postwar Effort

The end of World War II marked a new beginning for the Indy 500. The event had struggled gamely through the lean Depression years, only to be sidelined in 1942 in deference to the war effort. But when Tony Hulman bought the track in 1945, racing resumed the following May.

Fifty-eight entries appeared in Gasoline Alley for qualifying that year. Of them, only two were new: Lou Fageol's twin-engine, which Paul Russo slammed into the wall early in the race, and the powerful Novi owned by Lou Welch. The Novi was equipped with a supercharged 180-cubic-inch V-8 engine and a chassis designed and built by Frank Kurtis. The energy given off by this spectacular machine as it screamed down the straightaways made the hairs on the back of my neck tingle. Driver Ralph Hepburn and the Novi set a new track record of over 133 mph.

Deprived of Indy racing for almost five years, the fans turned out in record numbers, clogging streets for miles around the Speedway. I had never seen such a crowd, let alone a 500-mile race. And here I was, announcing the event for the first time. I worked from the top of the old Oriental-style pagoda behind the starting line, where it was almost impossible to see the action. Somehow I survived the day, although it took a dozen years at Indy before I began to feel comfortable with the Speedway's cast of thousands.

The Novi went out just after the halfway mark, and at the checkered flag only eight cars were still running. But racing was back, and the fans loved it. In the end, George Robson took command and nosed out Jimmy Jackson from Indianapolis. Later that year, Robson was killed while racing in Atlanta.

1947: Crossed Signals

Every driver comes to Indy knowing that at any moment, without warning, something can go wrong. But when personal error costs a driver the race, he never really gets over the disappointment. Certainly Bill Holland will never forget the bizarre ending of the 1947 Indy. Car owner Lou Moore entered two identical Blue Crown Specials in the second race of the postwar era—one driven by Holland, a rookie, and the other by veteran Mauri Rose. Both cars performed superbly, and at the 400-mile mark were running one-two. Holland had almost a full lap lead on Rose as they headed toward the finish line. But unfamiliar with the special driver's scoreboard at the starting line, Holland figured he had a full lap-plus lead on his teammate. So when owner Lou Moore gave both drivers the "E-Z" signal on the pit boards late in the race, Holland responded by dropping his speed by almost three miles per hour.

With twenty laps to go, Holland still led by a half-minute. Rose, sensing a chance at victory, picked up his speed and ran flat out, passing Holland without a challenge on Lap 193. Thinking he was still a full lap in front, Holland waved his teammate on with a salute. One lap later, Holland, still unaware of what had happened, trailed by twenty-four car lengths. It wasn't until Rose pulled into Victory Lane that Holland realized his error.

Two years later, again driving for Lou Moore, Holland won the 500. Even the sweetness of a well-deserved victory didn't erase the disappointment of his first start at the Speedway.

1967: A Controversial Entry

A newly designed and highly controversial turbine-powered race car, created by the rotund Andy Granatelli of STP fame, appeared in the 1967 lineup. Powered by twin Pratt & Whitney Aircraft engines, the new machine was quickly dubbed "The Silent Screamer." The turbine engine differed radically from the internal combustion engines that have long dominated racing. Rumors had it that the turbine would run on anything combustible—from perfume to Jack Daniels. In truth, the engines were fueled with kerosene.

The space-age engine caused quite a stir in the pits. Some competitors envied the powerful new engine and realized that nothing short of a miracle could stand between Granatelli's driver, Parnelli Jones, and the winner's circle. "There's no way we can keep Parnelli and the turbocar from winning," conceded Dan Gurney. Mario Andretti, who qualified faster than Parnelli, echoed Gurney's concern: "The rest of us will be racing for second place." Other competitors challenged the legality of the turbine. "It's just a damn airplane. It ain't no car and it just don't belong here," charged A.J. Foyt, the outspoken Texan.

Jones, who qualified sixth fastest among the thirty-three starters, quickly proved the superiority of the STP Special, as well as his ability to control a powerful machine at high speeds. He shattered one speed record after another and took the lead. It looked like an easy victory for Jones, but Mother Nature was not in a cooperative mood. Rain began to fall as Jones headed into Lap 18. The race was postponed until the next morning.

Again, Jones and the turbine-powered monster dominated the race, leading 171 of 200 laps. After 190 laps it seemed obvious that Jones would take the checkered flag. The crowd cheered the Speedway's first turbine car. Suddenly, I spotted Number 40 coasting to the infield just past the fourth turn. "Jones is out of power," I screamed into the public-address system. The crowd rose to its feet to watch the STP Special limp into the pits.

Just seven-and-a-half miles from victory, a ball bearing in the transmission had failed.

Jones was now out of the race and A.J. Foyt assumed the lead. With one lap to go, Foyt got the white flag, signaling the final lap. He maneuvered the Number 14 Sheraton-Thompson through the first three turns and headed for Turn Four. Seconds later the area erupted with spinning and crashing machines. Amid billowing puffs of smoke and dust we could see wheels flying in every direction. I lost sight of Foyt, who I thought had to be one of three machines tangled up on Turn Four.

"Where is he? Where is he? Where is he?" I shouted into the loudspeaker. "There he is. There he is. There he is." Miraculously, Foyt had pulled down deep in toward the infield, shifted into first gear, and dodged the three spinning cars, pieces of which littered the track. Flooring the Coyote chassis, Foyt took the checkered flag from starter Pat Vidan for his third victory at Indy.

Later that year, the United States Auto Club limited turbines in race cars to twenty-three square inches of inlet annulus area, then reduced that to just under sixteen inches in 1968. Granatelli waged a tough legal battle, but the court upheld the right of the sanctioning authority to set its own rules. A turbine with far less power, driven by Joe Leonard, came within nine laps of victory the following year. In 1975 the Cosworth V-8 engine, manufactured in England, appeared in Indy lineups and rapidly became the dominant source of power in all championship race cars.

1973: A Finish without Glory

If the 1967 race provided the most stirring ending, the 1973 event was memorable simply because it seemed it would never be completed. Under dark gray skies, the race started on May 28 with Johnny Rutherford in the coveted pole position. No sooner had the green flag dropped than Salt Walther crashed. Eleven other cars were caught in the pileup and the race was stopped. The clouds darkened as the track was cleared and before the race could resume, it started raining. The Indy was postponed until Monday morning.

Day Two brought more threatening weather. On the second parade lap, it was raining so hard that USAC officials cancelled the event until Tuesday morning. Thousands of race fans left the Speedway for the trek home. Airline reservations and other travel plans could not be changed; many had to return to work. Area restaurants had long since run out of box lunches. Trash was piling up everywhere; chicken bones, uneaten sandwiches and tons of paper cluttered the stands and infield. The place smelled like a city dump. We gathered early on the third day, but showers once more delayed the scheduled start.

Shortly after two p.m. the race resumed. On the fifty-seventh lap, Swede Savage crashed immediately after leaving the pits. The blazing fire brought out the red flag. Savage was taken to the hospital, where he died of severe burns several days later.

By now, most of us just wanted the ill-fated event to end. After waiting more than an hour for the Savage accident to be cleared, the race resumed. Gordon Johncock had the lead, but the rain halted the race again on Lap 133. Since the race is considered to have been run when half of it—one hundred laps—is completed and Gordie was in the lead, he was declared the winner—his first Indy victory. But even the victory ceremonies were cancelled because of the weather. Johncock was robbed of his moment of glory. Savage's accident and the rains proved to be a bigger story than Johncock's win.

1982: Duel to the Finish

Two superb drivers and two Cosworth engines made the 1982 finish the closest in Speedway history. Veteran racer Gordon Johncock and newcomer Rick Mears each represented top teams: Mears drove for Roger Penske, Johncock for Pat Patrick.

After both men completed their final pit stops,

Mauri Rose

Johncock had a ten-second lead over Mears at 190 laps, just twenty-five miles from the finish line. I asked the timers working with me to record time differences between the pair for the remaining ten laps. At 192 laps, Mears had narrowed the margin to eight seconds. The crowd began to sense, as I did, that Mears was preparing for a serious charge. Rick gained a full one-and-a-half seconds the next time around. Just six laps from the finish, Johncock's lead had dwindled to six seconds. Johncock was racing at 193 mph; Mears at 199 mph. Mears had an excellent shot at winning.

Four laps to go, Mears was just three seconds behind Johncock. The fans went wild. No one made a move for the exits. The next time around, Mears picked up another full second. Tom Sneva, in third at this point, slowed down, his machine smoking badly. We feared that the yellow flag would be waved to slow the field. It wasn't, and the duel continued.

On Lap 198, Mears neared the 200-mph mark— enough speed to get him around Johncock. He was only a half-second behind as the two charged across the finish line. On the white flag lap, Johncock kept the lead coming out of Turn Four. Mears swung to the outside as they shot down the main straightaway, hoping to "slingshot" past Johncock in the style made famous by NASCAR's best stock-car drivers. But the wily Johncock refused to give way and edged into the first turn just barely in front. Mears had to lift off his accelerator for an instant to get safely through the turn.

Going into the final lap, Mears set up for the pass at Turn Four. Johncock moved to the center, leaving Mears no time and little track to complete the pass. Starter Duane Sweeney waved the checkered flag at Johncock, with Mears trailing by just sixteen-hundredths of a second, by far the closest—and the most exciting—finish ever.

Inexorably, as history marches on, styles pass. The cast of drivers changes. Automotive technology races headlong towards the future. Yet the jewels of Indy's precious past (right) still glitter with timeless beauty.

In auto racing there is an abiding commitment to ruthless necessity—race-car design is an amalgam of hard-earned experience, fearless experiment, fierce optimism.

Through history, one of its most consistent, and perhaps surprising, products has been machinery of exquisite beauty. Time and again, a car that has been designed to withstand brutal punishment, to have its components abused to the outer limits of their endurance, somehow emerges as an object of eternal appeal.

From the days of Marmons and Loziers, through Peugeots and Duesenbergs and Millers, to Maseratis, Kurtises and Watsons, to today's March, Lola, Penske and Eagle, racing fans have flocked to Indy by the millions, seeking the same endlessly handsome spectacle— beautiful race cars being driven beautifully fast.

The spine-rattling war cry of racing engines at full power blasting around the bends, roaring up the straightaways fills the mind with images of racers past. Brave men, hundreds of them, have charged up these same straightaways, around these same bends. The garages and the pits and the turns are haunted with the spirits of the timeless ones— Harroun, DePalma, DePaolo, Meyer, Cummings, Shaw, Vukovich, Clark, Hill, Donohue.

At Indy, the past isn't gone. Every minute it's there in the shadows . . . watching, waiting . . . wanting to know how fast they'll go next lap.

1936

1912

1911▲ 1949▼

1911▲ 1919▼

Over decades, the shape of cars has changed, the look of photographs is different, but nothing of fundamental importance has changed.

Ever since 1911, when Louis Disbrow's Number 5 Pope led row two around on the pace lap prior to the start of the first Indy 500 (middle row, far left), crowds have gathered in the hundreds of thousands to watch the electrifying spectacle of the start. In 1928 and 1930, it was the same marvelous spectacle.

And since the beginning, there have been brave soldiers who struggled with futility. Though he would win the race eight years later, in 1911 Howdy Wilcox battled his Number 21 National (middle row, second from left) all race long, but only managed to move from his nineteenth-place start to a fourteenth-place finish.

Since the beginning, pit stops have been an essential part of the 500. In 1913 the crew changed a tire as driver Willie Haupt leaned against his Mason, built by the soon-to-be-famous Duesenberg brothers.

1928

1930

1913▲ 1957▼

1927▲ 1961▼

Racing at Indy has always meant danger. When Norman Batten's 1927 Miller burst into flame along the pit lane, he heroically guided it safely to the end of the pits. He was unhurt.

In 1949 Duke Nalon was less lucky. On Lap 23, a rear axle broke on his Novi in Turn Three; Nalon crashed and was seriously burned. In 1919 Jean Chassagne's Ballot went over the same wall. In 1957 not much had changed—the track was strewn with wreckage.

The photographs are old, the cars outdated, yet they're all unmistakably racing cars, all unmistakably hell-bent on going faster and farther than the rest. In 1911, 1928 or 1999, the challenge remains the same, the risks remain great. Whether the scorekeepers are seated in the old Pagoda (top row, far left) or the Speedway's modern control tower (bottom row, far right), the racers have always been driven by the same goals—to

One thing, however, has changed: Indy is no longer paved in brick, so it isn't necessary for the Speedway "technicians" (seen in 1961) to go over the track getting the dust out of the cracks with vacuum cleaners.

At Indianapolis the formula has been clear since the beginning—innovate or fail.

In 1911 Ray Harroun's Marmon Wasp was not the fastest car on race day. But Harroun was a clever, thoughtful racer. When his car came to the grid, a well-crafted frame was affixed to its cockpit containing a mirror (below).

It was the first automotive rearview mirror in history—a piece of safety equipment considered indispensable to the driving public ever since. Using this breakthrough device, Harroun went on to win the first Indy 500 at a speed of 74.59 mph.

Since 1911, the classic front-engine Indy car received refinement after refinement until the front-engine machine reached its highest form during the mid-1960s.

Lloyd Ruby's 1964 A.J. Watson roadster (below), with its powerful Offy engine set to the left and "laid down" in order to lower the car's center of gravity, was fast enough to bring Ruby home third.

But this was the last year that a front-engine car would win Indy. Already, the relentless march of innovation had brought modern rear-engine cars to the Speedway.

In the peaceful 1950s, while racing innovations were taking place elsewhere that would change Indy forever, during this quiet ▮▮▮ude the Speedway was a world unto itself.

The so-called "roadsters" of the 1950s had gotten lower and slightly wider t▮▮ heir forebears, but they still rolled comfortably into the same narrow garage bays that had housed the Indy cars of the 1920s. Their engines were still up front. Driveshafts still ran down the length of the chassis through the cockpit to the rear wheels.

What had once been round fuel drums bolted to the rear frame now became molded, handsomely fabricated teard▮▮ fuel tanks—but they were still mounted where they'd always been, at the rear of the frame.

The heavy old-style steel-beam chassis of 1911 had, by the 1950s, become a light, strong tubular "space-frame" chassis.

No racing mechanic from the first Indy 500 in 1911 would have had the least trouble identifying these 1957 cars. They were immediately recognizable, if vastly improved, versions of the racers from his own era. He might've had to think for a moment, however, to identify the Offy cylinder head (below)—though it is directly descended from the engine design of the 1913 Indy-winning Peugeot.

Since the first time a racer was second fastest, the question has been the same— if someone else is going faster, why can't I?

In 1957 driver Johnny Tolan, leaning on his Kuzma-Offy roadster (left), and chief mechanic Ernie Casale try to figure it out. They've qualified thirty-first and are in danger of being "bumped." What to do, what to do?

Sometimes the answer is technological: The engine isn't producing enough horsepower—we should change the cam, change the compression ratio, alter the fuel mixture.
The chassis isn't handling— we should change the suspension geometry, try different shock absorbers, another swaybar.
The car has too much drag down the straightaway—we'll cut down the windshield, block off some of the open ducts in the bodywork.

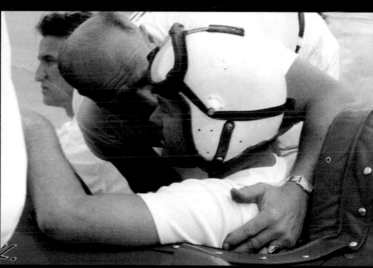

But sometimes the issue isn't technological. Sometimes it's the driver. Whether the car is right or not, the driver has only one duty, to drive it to the very limits of control— and then bring it back again.

The moments before qualification are the loneliest in an Indy driver's life. Nothing stands between him and success now except his own courage and skill. Will he get every bit of speed from the car, or will he make a mistake and demand too much?

In 1957 a concerned George Amick (top) thinks it over before going out to qualify. His concern was warranted —he missed the race.

Seated in his 1957 Kurtis-Kraft wearing only a T-shirt —those were the days—Bill Cheesbourg (below) gets last-minute encouragement . . . and qualifies twenty-third fastest.

Race day. The sights are familiar. Vast throngs waiting for the race.

There is a rain shower. It passes, and track crewmen pitch in to push standing water off the track at the entrance to the pit lane, so that the race can get under way.

Timers, scorers and officials fill the old Pagoda, prepared to keep a record of every car in the race, how many laps it has scored, when it pits, where it finishes.

Nurses from the infield hospital watch along the fence at Turn One, hoping they'll not be needed during the afternoon . . . perhaps secretly believing otherwise.

From home-built scaffolds, spectators in the infield ready themselves for the start of the race. Following a tragic scaffolding collapse during the 1960 race in which two were killed and twenty-two injured, all scaffolds are now banned from the Speedway.

Gradually, the race builds to its climax. In the 1956 race, the pit board of the John Zink team signals driver Pat Flaherty, leading the race, that he's on Lap 198—two more to go.

Chests swelling with triumph, owner and pit crew of the winning car erupt in celebration as their car crosses the finish line.

In 1956 starter Bill Vanderwater flags the Offy roadster of Gene Hartley through its qualifying run. First, the green flag signals that the run has officially begun.

After Hartley finishes three of his four qualifying laps, he's given the white flag—one lap to go.

Finally, the crowd on its feet, Vanderwater flashes the checkered flag. The qualifying run is complete. Better still, Hartley has made the show.

1953 Ernie McCoy

1961 Parnelli Jones

1962 Rodger Ward▲   1967 Parnelli Jones▼

1964 A.J. Foyt▲   1968 Bobby Unser▼

Regardless of how innovative, powerful and well-prepared a car is, to be successful it will always need one other crucial component—a Great Driver.

Through the 1950s and 1960s, Indy-car technology changed rapidly and dramatically, moving from front-engine racers directly derived from dirt-track sprint cars, through low, sleek Offy roadsters, to Grand Prix- inspired rear-engine cars, to radical turbine cars and the wedge-shaped all-American rear-engine Indy cars.

During this same period, the drivers piloting these difficult beasts comprised a breathtaking list of Indy heroes. They included Ernie McCoy in the 1953 Chapman-Offy, Parnelli Jones, winner A.J. Foyt and third-place finisher Rodger Ward—all in 1961 roadsters.

Using the same roadster again in 1962, Ward was the winner, while in 1964 A.J. Foyt managed the last win ever for a front-engine car.

The following season, the great Grand Prix champion Jim Clark took his Lotus-Ford to victory in his second Indy 500. A year later, fast-rising Grand Prix star Jackie Stewart was not so lucky, dropping out in his Lola-Ford while leading with only twenty-five miles to go.

1961 A.J. Foyt

1961 Rodger Ward

1965 Jim Clark▲ 1969 Jim McElreath▼

1966 Jackie Stewart▲ 1969 Mario Andretti▼

In 1967 Parnelli Jones's radical turbine car came even closer, leading with only four laps to go, when its turbine went dead. But the following year, Bobby Unser did everything right and brought his turbocharged-Offy Eagle home in first place.

In 1969 Jim McElreath's Offy caught fire on the front straight after only twenty-four laps, but Mario Andretti's Brawner Hawk-Ford was first to the checkered flag—surprisingly, it has been the brilliant but ill-starred Andretti's only Indy win.

Meanwhile, the vanquished lick their wounds. In 1955 an exhausted Ray Crawford (overleaf), fatigue and dejection etched deep in his face, sits in his racer. After 111 laps, his Offy has broken a va___. His 500 is finished.

There is no exhaustion in Victory Lane. The body may be dehydrated, the hands blistered. The shoulders and chest may ache from hour after hour of punishing battle with a raging race car.

The ears may be dulled from the cumulative blast of millions of deafening combustion pulses racing through the open exhaust pipe inches away . . . the clothing may be grimy, soaked through with sweat. . . .

But in Victory Lane there is no exhaustion . . . there will be time for that later.

For Bill Vukovich in 1954 (left) and Bob Sweikert in 1955 (right, greeted by a radio announcer and Dinah Shore), there is only the flush of triumph. In all of racing, there is no moment finer, higher, grander than this. It's a moment beyond fatigue, beyond excitement . . . beyond imagining.

The great crowd files out again, headed back to the day-to-day routine of the real world. Yet this vision they've witnessed—of great striving against enormous odds, of performing bravely and wisely in the midst of mortal danger—will bring the crowds back year after year. The drivers will come and go, the cars will evolve ever closer to the ideal, but the throngs of racing fans will always be there to greet them, to cheer them on, to stand and wave in their moment of triumph.

And when the great flood-tide of humanity recedes, the Speedway is quiet again.

But already, it is gathering itself for next year. They will return, all of them, the people, the cars, the excitement and drama . . . the trash, the beer cans, the torn paper cups.

Superteams

Starter Duane Sweeney enthusiastically waved the checkered flag as Danny Sullivan crossed the row of bricks at the finish line to win the 1985 Indianapolis 500. A roar welled up from the 400,000 spectators as the handsome Sullivan toured the oval on his victory lap. But it was as Sullivan headed down pit row to Victory Lane that the true spirit of racing showed itself: The members of the other teams broke into cheers. Each member of those thirty-two other teams was deeply disappointed that their own driver hadn't won. But as Sullivan, who had won it all in his third try at the Speedway, cruised by, that feeling was forgotten in a loud enthusiastic salute to the winner.

That spirit has long been a trademark of the men who prepare the machines and the men who race them. Although each team aims to win, in the competition there is cooperation. A team that is fresh out of engines can usually get another team's spare. A team whose car has been damaged in an accident can usually get the vital parts needed to rebuild from its competitors. The drivers willingly share knowledge of the Speedway's intricacies with their fellows.

Despite this very real and supportive camaraderie, however, the secrets of speed—how to get it and how to maintain it—are closely guarded. The equipment used by the top teams is virtually identical, March chassis and Cosworth engines. It is what happens after the chassis and engine are delivered to a team's shop that creates the small differences in speed that are the margin of victory. The reliance on engineering and on advanced aerodynamics to create that margin means that the teams with large financial resources most often find the keys to victory.

These highly successful teams resemble well-run corporations. But their product doesn't come off an assembly line. A modern racing machine is a sophisticated, delicate creation that is the result of individual knowledge and experimentation. When it's finished, it's put on a track where its fortunes are decided by racing luck, the skill of the driver, efficiency in the pits, accidents and dozens of elusive variables. It makes for unpredictable scenarios, both for the fans and for the teams themselves. In recent years, three teams bearing the names Penske, Cotter and Patrick have been highly successful at Indianapolis.

Penske Racing

With five Indy wins in two decades, the racing team owned by Roger Penske is the most formidable in the Speedway's long history. There is every reason to expect that dominance to continue. The success is due largely to the personal leadership of Roger Penske and his uncanny ability to pick drivers who fit his mold, and then bring them from obscurity to national prominence.

Rick Mears had precious little championship racing experience when Penske invited him to join the team. Starting with sprint buggies in the Mojave Desert near his home in Bakersfield, California, Rick had graduated to off-road races and competition at Pike's Peak. The move from off-road to the oval track was a big one. "I was in the right place at the right time," Rick explained. "Former Speedway driver Wally Dallenbach organizes a motorcycle expedition in the Colorado Rockies each fall, and in 1977, I was invited along. There were thirty-three riders, including Roger Penske. We rode about 125 miles a day for four days, stopping at night. One morning we were outside of a hotel getting ready to go when Roger walked up and said he had an offer. He said if I was interested to give him a call. Needless to say, I didn't argue with him."

In addition to Mears, Penske has chosen other unknown drivers: Mark Donohue, Danny Sullivan,

Tom Sneva and Kevin Cogan. Mixing their talents with veterans Bobby and Al Unser and Mario Andretti produced not only the five Indianapolis titles but a string of national driving championship titles as well.

Roger picks drivers not only because he feels they have potential, but also for their ability to test drive, to make a sharp public appearance, to mix graciously with sponsors, and to avoid trouble on a race track.

Rick Mears

Mears has never driven at Indy for anyone but Roger Penske. But he's done that very, very well, bringing home two wins in less than a decade. Rick captured the pole position the second year he entered, 1979, driving the Gould Charge to an average qualifying speed of almost 194 mph. Mears battled his teammate, Bobby Unser, and A.J. Foyt late in the race, but Unser and Foyt had engine problems. Mears led the final nineteen laps and took the checkered flag. Running behind Mears, Foyt's engine expired on the final lap. The fans went berserk when they saw A.J. crawling out of Turn Four, out of power, with the number three and four cars on his tail. We all wondered if he'd make it to the finish line before someone passed him. It seemed to take an eternity for Foyt's car to roll down the straightaway and cross the yard of bricks to take second place.

The 1979 victory exemplified Mears's driving philosophy. "The desert racing taught me to stay out of trouble," he said. "When you race off-road down in Mexico you have one lap that's 800 miles long. You don't know the terrain: You have to run what's in front of you, and you've got to get to the end. That taught me that you've got to finish a race before you can do anything. To finish first, first you must finish—that's what it all boils down to. It's really paid off. At Indianapolis, when you're running the length of a football field every second, you simply can't afford to make a mistake."

Fire Storm

A mistake did happen in the 1981 race. It wasn't on the race track, but in the pits, and Rick was an innocent victim. During a pit stop, fuel began pouring from the fuel hose before it was properly mated to the filler neck on the car's fuel tank. Fuel poured over the car, down over Mears, and into the engine compartment, bursting into flames.

"All I could think of was to get out of the car and get away," Mears said, remembering the incident. "I was on fire from the waist up. Once out of the car, I couldn't breathe. Being on fire and burning was one thing, but not being able to breathe was the part that got to me. I ran around the front of the car. Somebody tried to take my helmet off. I had my eyes shut because the fire was trying to burn my eyes too. But he couldn't get the helmet off because the fire was burning his hand. So I waited a moment, opened my eyes, and saw a fireman with an extinguisher. I ran, jumped over the wall in front of him, and grabbed the fire extinguisher. When I did, it evidently caught him on fire. He didn't have protective clothing, so he dropped the extinguisher and fled. By that time, my dad was there. He grabbed the extinguisher and put the fire out."

The pit fire destroyed the Penske machine and sent Mears and several crew members to the hospital. Although he underwent a series of skin grafts to repair the damage, those who know about the fire can still detect faint traces of the disaster on Rick's face.

After such a dreadful experience, Mears came right back. The next year, 1982, he set new one-lap and four-lap qualifying records and earned the pole position for the second time. His fastest qualifying lap was 207.612 mph and his average for the ten-mile run was better than 207 mph. During the race, he turned in the fastest single lap, 200.535 mph in traffic. At the close of the race, Rick dueled with Gordon Johncock in the kind of action that legends are made of. Johncock nosed out Mears by just sixteen-hundredths of a second. Despite missing his chance to repeat as the winner at Indianapolis,

Mears went on to capture his third national driving title that season. Rick got his second Indy victory in 1984. He took the checkered flag easily, beating runner-up Roberto Guerrero by two laps.

Strike Two

They say that lightning never strikes the same spot twice, but Mears suffered another crippling blow in September 1984, while practicing for a race in Quebec, Canada. Attempting to pass Bobby Rahal, Mears chopped across the front of another car driven by Corrado Fabi. Mears crashed into the guardrail separating the track from the pit lane. The impact tore out a retaining post, and the guardrail sliced right through the front bulkhead of the car. The champion's badly damaged feet were sticking out of the front of the car when it finally came to a halt.

Rick was flown to Methodist Hospital in Indianapolis, where Dr. Terry Trammel began reconstructing Mears's feet. The doctor had to reattach both Achilles tendons using a latticework of screws and pins. It was fifteen long weeks before all of the hardware could be removed. Released from Methodist Hospital in December, Mears began the long process of rehabilitation. He had to give up road racing for the 1985 season because the constant clutching and gear-shifting it requires were too much for his feet. Al Unser took over the Mears road-racing machine and drove it to a national championship.

There are a dozen things that can cause a race car to go out of control on a track, and it would have been easy enough for Mears to say he'd hit a spot of oil or his tires had slipped. But Rick maintains to this day that the accident in Canada was his own fault. "There were circumstances that caused it, but it wasn't anybody's fault," he said. "It was my fault for putting myself in that position." Being honest, being willing to admit driving mistakes is the mark of a great driver.

Rick's confident stride and effervescent personality indicated he had completely recovered when the Indy season began in May 1986. A bright yellow Pennzoil Z-7 Special responded to Rick's enthusiasm. First came new track records, 217.581 mph for a single lap and 216.828 mph for the ten-mile run, securing a pole position. Rick's skilled command of the March chassis had him leading 77 of the 200 laps. Despite handling problems in traffic, Rick chased Bobby Rahal and Kevin Cogan to the finish, only 1.84 seconds behind the winner at the end of 500 miles.

Danny Sullivan

The gods of racing were certainly riding with Mears's teammate Danny Sullivan during his 1985 victory at Indianapolis. Mario Andretti was leading just past the halfway point with Sullivan in relentless pursuit. He had been closing in on Andretti for a dozen laps, and then made his move to take the lead. Danny began to pass right at the end of the main stretch and ducked inside of Andretti going into Turn One. Here were two drivers going side by side through a turn at 200 mph. Neither backed off. Passing below the normal racing line, or "groove," Sullivan's machine suddenly started to spin—the kind of mishap that usually ends up with the car finding the concrete wall on the outside of the track. Mario kept his foot on the throttle and veered to the left of the spinning Sullivan. As luck would have it, Sullivan did a perfect 360-degree loop and found himself pointed right into Turn Two. Obviously, Sullivan had no direct control over the car during the spin, it was just "his day."

The action brought out the yellow light and both Andretti and Sullivan headed for the pits. Mario stopped only for fuel, while Sullivan required a complete change of tires. When they emerged from the pit road, Andretti was still leading and Sullivan was again chasing him. The fans knew that Sullivan had to make another move to pass Andretti. Sullivan picked the same spot on the track to try again, heading into Turn One, but this time the pass was clean. Danny captured the lead on the 140th lap

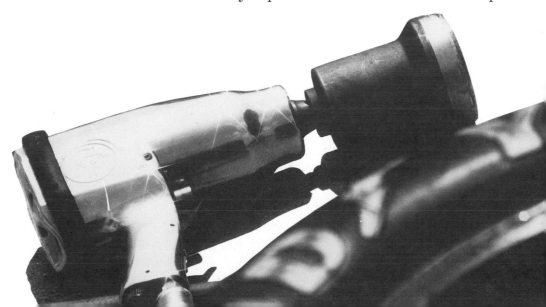

COTTER RACING CAR STARTUP

INDY CARS

2 Complete Cars	$338,000
6 Motors	300,000
Motor Spares	75,000
16 Clutches	10,400
8 Sets 4-Wheels	20,800
22 Wide Gear Ratios	8,690
115 Narrow Gear Ratios	23,000
45 Brake Pad Sets	6,300
9 Ring & Pinions	13,500
1 Gear Box	25,000
4 Front Uprights	26,000
4 Rear Uprights	26,000
4 Front Shocks	8,000
4 Rear Shocks	8,000
1 Steering Box	975
3 Front Roll Bars	3,600
3 Rear Roll Bars	2,025
2 Front Speedway Wings	2,000
2 Rear Speedway Wings	8,000
2 Front Short Track Wings	2,000
2 Rear Short Track Wings	8,000
Body Work	30,000
4 Headers	21,600
Page 1 Total	$966,890

PIT EQUIPMENT

1 CART Fuel Tank	$3,000
1 Speedway Fuel Tank	7,500
2 Tow Carts	10,000
5 Wheel Guns	1,500
6 Wheel Sockets	1,200

TEAM SAFETY EQUIPMENT

8 Firesuits	1,600
12 Team Uniforms	5,000
2 Helmets	300

TRANSPORTATION

1 Tractor	75,000
1 Trailer	115,000
Trailer Equipment	25,000
1 One Ton Truck	21,000
1 Pickup	13,000
1 Van	15,000
Page 2 Total	$294,100

BUILDING INVENTORY

1	Dynomometer	$250,000
2	Drill Presses	3,800
1	Large Metal Break	12,000
1	Small Metal Break	5,000
2	Shears	13,000
2	Welders	6,000
1	Cherry Picker	400
1	Hoist	900
1	Magnaflux	5,500
1	Air Compressor	3,000
5	Parts Washers	6,000
1	Lathe & Tooling	15,000
1	Mill & Tooling	16,000
1	Band Saw	9,500
	Electronic Scales	11,000
	Surface Grinders	6,500
12	Work Benches	4,800
	Nut & Bolt Inventory	5,500
	Aero Quip Fittings & Hose	11,000
1	Oven	1,200
1	High Pressure Parts Washer	3,000
1	Valve Grinder	5,000
3	Engine Stands	1,200
2	Chassis Dollies	900
2	Gear Box Stands	800
	Page 3 Total	$397,000

SHOW CARS

2 Show Cars $40,000

OFFICE EQUIPMENT

Furniture &
Equipment
                                  7,500

CART PROPERTIES
                                 60,000

ALARM SYSTEMS
                                  5,000

Page 4 Total	$	112,500
Page 3 Total	$	397,000
Page 2 Total	$	294,100
Page 1 Total	$	966,890
GRAND TOTAL		$1,770,490

and was untouchable the rest of the way, turning laps in traffic at better than 200 mph.

With his matinee-idol looks, Sullivan appeared later that year in an episode of NBC's *Miami Vice*, playing a race driver accused of murder. For this dramatic debut, Sullivan hired an acting coach. But at the Speedway, Sullivan needs no coach; obviously, he has learned his driving lessons well.

Penske Power

Sullivan's win made Roger Penske the most successful car owner in the Speedway's history. He combines two basic ingredients—work and money—to create well-deserved success. Roger spends the entire month of May at Indianapolis. He's up at six a.m. each day jogging on the Speedway's infield golf course. Then he works with his team into the night in Gasoline Alley. Penske's team, which usually enters three cars at Indianapolis, is always dressed immaculately. Under the watchful eye of team manager Derrick Walker, a quiet Scotsman, the entire operation displays Penske's passion for perfection.

Although Roger presides over a huge business empire, which includes truck leasing and Penske Power, a heavy-equipment sales firm, he is closely involved with the racing operation headquartered in Reading, Pennsylvania. He's always ready to try a new idea. He unveiled a new engine to power his cars at Indianapolis in 1986. Called the Chevy Indy V-8, the 2.65-liter, turbocharged, double-overhead-cam V-8 is a product of a joint venture between Chevrolet, Penske and Ilmor Engineering of England. Penske is the first to use the new power plant in place of the traditional Cosworth. If Roger's eye for engines is as keen as his talent for finding drivers, other teams may one day have Penske power in their cars as well.

Team Cotter

For a newcomer to Indianapolis, Team Cotter Racing has a phenomenal record. In 1982, its first year of operation, Cotter finished fourth. The following year, Tom Sneva won the 500 carrying the Cotter colors. When Sneva joined another team, rookie Roberto Guerrero finished second in 1984, third in 1985, and fourth in 1986.

Owner Dan Cotter is the president of the nationwide True Value Hardware organization. An avid racer, his interest in competition was sparked in 1953. Though he was still in high school, Cotter bought a midget racer. Dan's father disapproved so strongly that Dan sold the midget and concentrated on his education, taking on the family business afterwards. The thrill of the track never left his mind, though, and in 1981 he went into partnership with legendary chief mechanic George Bignotti. Bignotti retired in 1985, selling his share of the team to Dan, who is now the sole owner.

Full Preparation

The Cotter Racing facility covers two-and-a-half acres in Indianapolis. Its headquarters alone has 17,000 square feet under one roof. Fifteen full-time employees keep the racing machines in top condition. Looking over the grounds, business manager Dennis Hardy indicated that the best does not come cheaply. "To start up an operation of this type would take an outlay of about four million dollars," he said. Dennis well remembers 1985, when his racing budget suffered a severe jolt. At the United States Grand Prix at the Meadowlands track in New Jersey, Guerrero totally wiped out two cars. "That was a half-million dollars shot right there," Hardy said. "I mean, those cars were wiped out. We brought the pieces back from New Jersey and put them in the dumpster out back."

Veteran chief mechanic Phil Casey oversees a shop filled with fabricating equipment, assembly bays, lathes, milling machines and a state-of-the-art dynamometer for engine development. The equipment and talent in the shop could build a brand new race car from the road up, but of course that would be very expensive.

Casey figures that the Team Cotter transporter alone costs as much as teams used to spent for an

George Bignotti (second from left) with Gordon Johncock, Wally Dallenbach and crewman

entire season of racing in the 1960s. The transporter is fitted with a lift gate, a powerful electrical generator, air conditioners and a 720-square-foot awning. Inside are two complete March cars, four Cosworth engines, a spare gearbox and six sets of wheels. Then there are five spare turbo units, three rear wings, three sets of front wings and extra gears, clutches and brakes. There's a welder, metal shear, lathe, bandsaw and a huge selection of hand tools. With this gear, the team is ready to recover from any accident short of a total wipe-out, such as those suffered at the Meadowlands.

Cotter Racing starts each new season with two new March chassis, nine Cosworth engines and three million dollars to spend. When spectators at Indianapolis see Roberto Guerrero nose up onto the starting grid, they're looking at better than a quarter of a million dollars rolling up to the line. That's quite a load of responsibility resting on the shoulders of the young driver, who was born in 1958, the same year that A.J. Foyt first raced at the Speedway.

Roberto Guerrero

With any kind of racing luck, Guerrero's fortunes could match those of the inimitable Foyt. A native of Colombia, Roberto's passion for racing is something that runs in his family. His father was born in Argentina and was an Olympic cyclist for that country, competing in the 1948 games in England. After moving to Colombia in the 1950s, the senior Guerrero began racing go-karts for fun. Roberto inherited his father's interest in speed, and by the time he was twelve years old had won two national go-kart championships.

Guerrero convinced his family that he should be educated in England. He'd be able to learn English, and he'd be able to attend the fine English schools. He was also angling to get into auto racing, and he figured his chances of doing so were far better in England than in Colombia. Just six months before taking his collegiate degree, Roberto attended an English race-driving school. He immediately got a

start and raced for two years in the Grand Prix Formula One series for the Ensign team. In 1983 Dan Cotter made a trip to England where he met and signed Guerrero, and Roberto made his first start at Indy in 1984, taking second place and sharing Rookie of the Year honors with Michael Andretti.

Oval Allure

During his stint with the Ensign road racing team, Guerrero had his eyes on a start at Indianapolis. Dan Cotter gave him the chance. But, as other European drivers have found, the transition from road courses to the oval track is not an easy one. Roberto believes that the strong rookie orientation program at Indianapolis, the availability of a month for practice, and the competence of the Cotter team were responsible for his exceptional showing in his first start. The showing might have been even better. As Dennis Hardy pointed out, Roberto actually spent less running time on the track than did the winner, Rick Mears. "It was the amazing pit stops of the Penske team that beat us."

Roberto describes the Indianapolis 500 in one word: "overwhelming." He always gets to the track early on race day, but secludes himself in his motor home near the garage area. Arriving at his car shortly before the start, he believes this routine helps him avoid hours of nervous anxiety. Once in the car, his mind is focused on the job at hand and there's no time for "butterflies."

On race day, Guerrero's cheering section includes his wife Katie, a Californian who met Roberto when he was competing at Monaco. Their son, Marco, arrived in 1985 and he'll soon be trackside. An Argentinian cyclist will be there as well. The senior Guerrero missed a gold medal in the Olympic games, but he believes his son will win the world's greatest racing prize, the Indianapolis 500.

Patrick Racing

The two-car Patrick Racing team is a prime example of an operation that thrives on excellent engineering. Long gone are the days when a chief mechanic, his helper and a driver hauled a single machine to the Speedway. At Patrick, twenty-four full-time employees work in an 18,000-square-foot complex that includes a machine shop and fabrication area, an engine room and an engineering and race preparation area.

At the beginning of each season, Patrick Racing purchases four new March chassis—the exact same chassis the other teams have bought from the English firm. Add the basic Cosworth racing engine and Patrick's racing package is essentially the same as everyone else's. But then the team manager, Jim McGee, goes to work. A youthful-looking veteran, McGee helped chief mechanic Clint Brawner put Mario Andretti in Victory Lane. Now McGee has a lot of talented help himself.

One of the most basic changes in the operation of racing teams came in 1980 with the addition of engineers. Patrick Racing employs three engineers to help make their March/Cosworth machines faster than anyone else's March/Cosworth machines. Tony Cicale is the chief engineer. A former professor at Cornell University who specializes in aerodynamics, Tony spends his time working on body shape, ground effects and other aerodynamic problems. Ed Nathman is a mechanical engineer who works with the car's machinery and its systems—the fuel system, the waste gate system, the electronic system. Peter Gibbons, a stress design engineer, has an MIT degree behind him and looks after weight, body panel stiffness and related matters. This trio is charged with finding the key to success for Patrick Racing. When the machines arrive at Indianapolis, they are ready to test the engineers' theories of speed, handling and reliablity.

Science and Art

Do these engineers and their computers minimize the role of the chief mechanic? McGee feels that fielding a car is still very much a team effort. The engineers draw their plans on paper, but they depend on the chief mechanic and his shop team to build it and make it work. The chief mechanic is still the focal point of the team; he's the one who supervises the final assembly of the pieces and the person who puts the man in the machine.

Race day decisions are the province of the chief mechanic as well. The work of the engineers has long been finished. Race strategy and pit stop decisions are made by team manager McGee for one car and by the team's owner, U.E. (Pat) Patrick for the other car. Patrick is a tough-minded oil wildcatter. He's in racing because he loves it. It's in his blood, and his fierce competitive drive demands he provide the team with the finest personnel, equipment and facilities.

Patrick's first team started Indianapolis in 1969 with Johnny Rutherford in the cockpit. Of the crop of drivers currently competing at the 500, at least twenty have driven for him. Driver Gordon Johncock has won Indianapolis twice for Patrick Racing. When current drivers Emerson Fittipaldi and Kevin Cogan answer the green flag at Indianapolis, they know that Patrick has given them, the fans and the sponsors an all-out professional effort. Both men have the skill to win; the only other thing they need is a share of racing luck.

There are other teams with the budget and the talent to earn successes at Indianapolis. The list includes Kraco with Michael Andretti; Galles Racing with Geoff Brabham, Pancho Carter and Roberto Moreno; Truesports with Bobby Rahal; Newman-Haas with Mario Andretti; and Shierson Racing with Al Unser Jr. These teams can win any race at any track at any time.

The field at Indianapolis, however, contains thirty-three machines, representing an average two-dozen teams. While there are many teams entered each year whose budgets are far slimmer than those of the superteams, their ambitions are just as lofty. And when the green flag drops, it's a race. Their hopes for victory are no less justified.

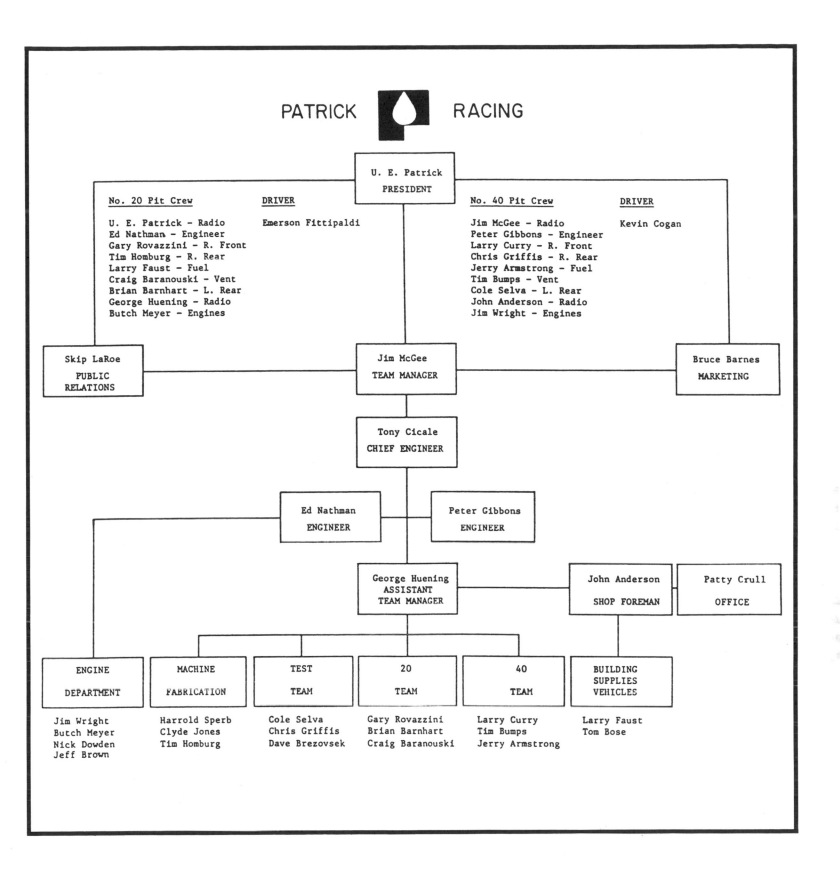

PATRICK RACING

U. E. Patrick
PRESIDENT

No. 20 Pit Crew

U. E. Patrick - Radio
Ed Nathman - Engineer
Gary Rovazzini - R. Front
Tim Homburg - R. Rear
Larry Faust - Fuel
Craig Baranouski - Vent
Brian Barnhart - L. Rear
George Huening - Radio
Butch Meyer - Engines

DRIVER

Emerson Fittipaldi

No. 40 Pit Crew

Jim McGee - Radio
Peter Gibbons - Engineer
Larry Curry - R. Front
Chris Griffis - R. Rear
Jerry Armstrong - Fuel
Tim Bumps - Vent
Cole Selva - L. Rear
John Anderson - Radio
Jim Wright - Engines

DRIVER

Kevin Cogan

Skip LaRoe
PUBLIC
RELATIONS

Jim McGee
TEAM MANAGER

Bruce Barnes
MARKETING

Tony Cicale
CHIEF ENGINEER

Ed Nathman
ENGINEER

Peter Gibbons
ENGINEER

George Huening
ASSISTANT
TEAM MANAGER

John Anderson
SHOP FOREMAN

Patty Crull
OFFICE

ENGINE DEPARTMENT	MACHINE FABRICATION	TEST TEAM	20 TEAM	40 TEAM	BUILDING SUPPLIES VEHICLES
Jim Wright	Harrold Sperb	Cole Selva	Gary Rovazzini	Larry Curry	Larry Faust
Butch Meyer	Clyde Jones	Chris Griffis	Brian Barnhart	Tim Bumps	Tom Bose
Nick Dowden	Tim Homburg	Dave Brezovsek	Craig Baranouski	Jerry Armstrong	
Jeff Brown					

Machinists Union Racing

"We have just as good a chance to win at Indianapolis as anybody." Confident? You bet. Based on reality? Positively. The man who made that statement is Andy Kenopensky, whose job as National Automotive Coordinator for 125,000 truck and auto mechanics in the United States and Canada puts him in command of a two-car team. Andy is friendly and full of enthusiasm, the perfect man to run a racing team.

Andy started his career as a diesel mechanic. Going to school at night and after work, he earned a B.S. from Cornell University and a master's degree in education from Rutgers. He's done well in the classroom, but he's right at home on the floor of the shop as well. His knowledge of suspension setups and gear changes equals that of his two chief mechanics.

"We can probably run a race team on what most of the big teams throw away." If that sounds like Andy pinching pennies on behalf of the union's members, it isn't. "We just buy what we need," he says. While he operates without a fixed budget, Kenopensky knows he has to be prudent and able to justify the ever-increasing cost of racing.

If the Machinists Union had unlimited funds, would it affect the operation? Probably. First, instead of buying two new March chassis each year, they would buy four. As it is, they must take their Indianapolis machines and completely rework them for the race in Milwaukee the following week. The superteams have a short-track racer and a long-track racer, plus backups, all set to go. Andy doesn't have that luxury. Instead, the ten employees work long hours resetting the cars for the next race on the schedule.

Then there's the matter of testing; it's just not in Andy's program. Big-budget teams lease the race courses, including Indianapolis, far in advance of a race to make certain that the car will be properly set up on race day. The Machinists Union goes to a track, takes a couple of hours to practice, then goes out to qualify.

For most races, that gives the superteams a big advantage. But at Indianapolis, that advantage is greatly diminished. The track is open to all entrants for the entire month of May. That gives the teams plenty of time to practice and to test, experiment and then test again.

Not all of the extras laid on by the superteams are a distinct advantage. Kenopensky says, "I honestly don't believe we're at a disadvantage because we don't have an engineer." Certainly there isn't much room to house an extra employee in the team's small race shop on the west side of Indianapolis. The team rents the space from generous Al Unser at "a very low figure."

With unions in the U.S. asking everyone to "Buy American," it does bother the Machinists Union that they're forced to field an English racing machine in order to be competitive. When they began operations in 1981, the team built their own car with an American engine, but it just couldn't keep up with the March/Cosworth entries. Andy hopes the day isn't too far off when an American chassis builder can equal the English March and Lola platforms. Andy keeps telling Dan Gurney to "build a competitive Eagle chassis so we can buy it."

Getting on Track

The Machinists Union first exhibited an interest in racing in 1978. That year, William Winpisinger, the president of the union, decided to sponsor a race at Trenton, New Jersey. A former auto mechanic, "Wimpy," as he is known to the union members, felt a national public-relations program built around auto racing would focus attention on the members' skills. The race team followed soon after. At their national convention in 1984, the union members voted to commend the racing team and continue the program. The team has a one-hour videotape of excerpts from live television coverage of the 1985 races that focused on the Union entry. "What would that kind of television coverage cost if we had to buy it?" Kenopensky asked.

The team's number-one driver is Josele Garza of

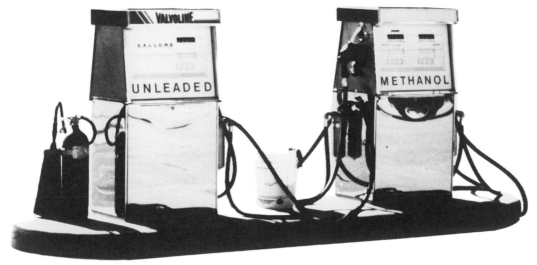

Mexico City. Garza was the first Latin American to qualify and start a race at Indianapolis, and he garnered the Rookie of the Year honors in 1981. The team has started a bit slowly, but has steadily climbed in the rankings, even leading some races. Andy Kenopensky knows the team is competitive, and figures that victories can't be far behind.

Morales Auto Sports

The state flag of New Mexico flies under the Stars and Stripes on a flagpole in front of the Morales racing headquarters in Indianapolis. The man in charge, Johnny Capels, is a native of Albuquerque and the type of rugged individualist who seems to thrive in the arid Southwest. Capels is both chief mechanic and team manager. The Morales team won the Michigan 500 in 1981 with driver Pancho Carter, and took the checkered flag at the Montreal 300 with Johnny Rutherford at the wheel. Capels is certain that Indianapolis, too, can be conquered.

Capels, a veteran of thirty-five years as a driver and mechanic, explained the team's philosophy of competition: "We'll do what we have to do. If our driver wipes us out of both race cars midway through the season, we'll still be at every race on the schedule because that's our job. We may have to dig up a coffee can somewhere and pull out the greenbacks to get us through, but we're not a team that pulls up short and quits."

That philosophy was put to a severe test in 1985. Three-time Indianapolis champion Rutherford wiped out a machine while leading the Pocono 500, and a severe crash at Phoenix wiped out another. Those two accidents cost the Morales team an extra quarter of a million dollars. But they survived, ran every event and bought two new March chassis for the 1986 campaign.

Speedway Dreams

Capels, who has been named mechanic of the year twice, dreams of a victory at Indianapolis. He knows full well what the infusion of nearly a half-million dollars in cash would do for the operation.

That's his big goal. It's far easier to sign sponsors for a team with an Indianapolis trophy in its headquarters.

Winning at Indy is not at all beyond the team's means. Capels believes their odds of winning are as good as anyone else's. Capels has a full-time work force of five mechanics, all of them with experience in midget and sprint cars. Capels is not only chief mechanic and team manager, he answers the telephone in the office, pays the bills, buys the equipment, handles the payroll, sets travel arrangements and secures the sponsors.

For the 1986 campaign, Morales Auto Sports had five Cosworth engines ready. Four of them were used and one was brand new. The new Cosworth cost $43,675. Once the season began, each engine was overhauled after 600 miles of competition. That's another $4,700, plus parts. The engine that tested the best on the dynamometer was the one put in the chassis for Rutherford at Indianapolis. Rutherford completed 198 laps, finishing eighth.

Owner Alex Morales provides inspiration for the team. Alex was born in 1909–two years before the first 500–and his first love is auto racing. Morales's company, Alex Foods, makes tortillas and other Mexican food products under the Piñata brand. But most of the time, you'll find him working on his sprint cars for competition at Ascot Park in California. He drops by the office for a few minutes each day, then heads for the garage to get the engines and chassis ready. Morales is always in Indianapolis for the race, down in the pits with his team. Like Capels, he has high hopes that one year his trips to the Speedway will wind up in Victory Lane.

The Chief of Chief Mechanics

It's the drivers, and perhaps the owners, who are the focus of attention at Indy. But everyone in racing knows just how crucial a team's chief mechanic—the "head wrench"—really is. And of all the chief mechanics who've worked their magic at

Indianapolis, none can match the brilliant record of George Bignotti. A quarter of a century at the 500 brought him seven wins. He's also the all-time leader in championship victories with eighty-four. No other chief is within forty-five of that total. Although George sold his interest in Cotter Racing in 1985, it would be no surprise to see him assemble another team and return to the Speedway.

George put A.J. Foyt in Victory Lane twice, in 1961 and 1964. Despite the victories, the volatile pair soon parted company. "He's brilliant, but he's always got to be the boss," explained Foyt. Bignotti's reply echoed Foyt's own words: "A.J. was getting to the point where he wanted to run the show instead of me. If we'd stayed together, we'd have won a lot of races."

George won a lot of races for every team he was on. Englishman Graham Hill won Indy for him in 1966. Al Unser won two consecutive victories, 1970 and 1971, in machines prepared by Bignotti. George did a turn with Patrick Racing, preparing the car that Gordon Johncock won with in 1973. The latest victory came in 1983, when Bignotti was a partner in Cotter Racing and Tom Sneva was his driver.

Through it all, George has been an expert at public relations. He thoroughly enjoys attending all of the race functions and is at home in front of a crowd or a live microphone. He was the one chief mechanic I could always count on for an interview regardless of how much pressure he was under. In a way, George and his devotion to excellence symbolize the very best of Indy.

In the first week of May they begin arriving. From Texas, California, Pennsylvania, Arizona, Florida, Canada—from all directions—they converge on the Indianapolis Motor Speedway, the great war-wagons of the racing teams. Jammed to capacity with every imaginable weapon of battle, these enormous long-haul rigs are more than mere transports. Deep in their polished and fresh-painted innards, they offer complete machine shops capable of producing all but the most fundamental of engine parts.

Most carry two complete race cars; some, even more. Spare engines and drivetrain parts are packed aboard in grand profusion. Countless sets of extra body parts and spare racing wheels, needed for the 500's seven or more pits stops, are carefully stored.

But the hardware will be of no use without the inclusion of one other key element—a full crew, complete with engineer, aerodynamicist, team manager, chief mechanic and a squadron of eager, energetic, knowledgeable mechanics. These "wrenches" are the lifeblood of a racing team. Without their dedicated expertise, the multimillion-dollar budgets that corporate sponsors lavish upon well-heeled Indy-car teams will only buy disorganization, frustration—and worst of all for the sponsor, the specter of public failure.

So for all the richness of their budgets and the enormous profusion of supplies available to them, there is extraordinary pressure upon the teams to perform, and perform spectacularly.

Nothing succeeds like success, the saying goes, but in auto racing it has a cruel bite. For it's a harsh fact that among first-line Indy teams, only total victory is success. Whether it's Spencer Wishart finishing second to winner Jules Goux in 1913 by 13 minutes, 8 seconds, or Rick Mears missing victory behind Gordon Johncock in 1982 by only 0.16 of a second, at Indy a "near win" is total defeat.

From the minute they arrive at the Speedway to begin painstaking preparation of the cars for the difficult test ahead, the teams feel extreme pressure to perform, to excel, to be perfect . . . to win.

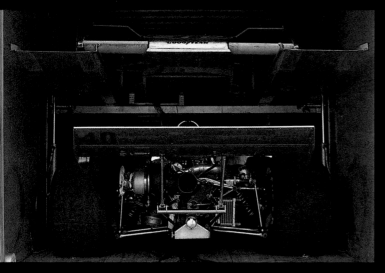

The mighty diesel rigs of the racing teams queue up in the Garage Area parking lot. Their precious cargo of racing cars is still sealed from the competition's prying eyes.

But even the trucks themselves are a feast for the discerning eye, especially the handsomely customized black-and-chrome Penske Racing "Super-Truck" (top row, right). Like so many knights' chargers, these immaculate transports wear the livery of the team's sponsor proudly emblazoned upon their flanks.

After the teams have scrubbed and polished their garages until they are clean as a surgeon's theater—for nothing distinguishes the professional racing mechanic more certainly than his attention to order, detail, absolute cleanliness— then one by one, the rolling weapons are unveiled.

Carefully the mechanics back them down the ramps out of the trucks. The gravel and grit of Gasoline Alley grumble under their fat racing tires for the first time.

Untested, expectant, bright with gleaming potential, at last they are on the field of battle. But there is no time now for testing the turf. Immediately, the serious work begins. First, the cars undergo routine teardowns. Engines are separated from chassis, transmissions are separated from engines. Any key components that the team considers secret—such as Patrick Racing's 1983 rear wing (bottom row, second from left)—are carefully shrouded from view.

Every piece and particle of the car are inspected. At the least hint that a part is defective, worn, in any way less than perfect, it is thrown out and replaced.

Then, for what will be the first of many times during the month of May, all of the components are carefully reassembled. The awkward mountain of bits and pieces begins to assume the flowing shape of a race car again. Wheels and tires are checked. Wing settings are adjusted.

As the mechanics put the finishing touches to the car, preparing it for its first practice session on the track, the sponsor's Hospitality Area (bottom row, far right) is readied—for as well as it is a race, the Indy 500 is an intense public relations effort. A sponsor's identity can be enhanced just as effectively at the V.I.P. buffet as in the Garage Area.

There is far more to the Indy 500 than just assembling a race car—demanding as that alone may certainly be.

All other aspects of running a 500-mile race must be organized as well. The race-day refueling tanks, built to strict USAC design regulations, must have their interiors freshly scoured to insure that no impurities will find their way into the engine's fuel system.

The labor-saving tractors used to pull the cars to and from the pits during practice sessions must be kept in good working order. Indeed, all manner of time-consuming secondary tasks must be completed in order to keep the complex modern racing team moving smoothly ahead. From the first glimmer of dawn until late into the night, the work grinds on.

The first weekend of qualifying approaches and the drivers begin to press their cars. Mechanical problems start to surface.

The activity in the Garage Area (overleaf) becomes more intense. Engines blow up. Transmissions and clutches give way. Turbochargers melt down. Wheel-bearings seize.

Day and night the search for reliability . . . and always, more speed . . . goes on.

Suspensions are set, changed, set back to where they were before. The juggling of components takes on a dizzying quality.

Yet amidst the confusion, there is always one car, as yet unknown, that will warrant the struggle. In 1982 it was Gordon Johncock's eventual winner (overleaf, bottom row, right), here being ministered to in the early days of practice by "head wrench" George Huening.

Each team's garage door is a bulletin board. Prominently displayed will be the car's qualifying speed—provided the team is lucky enough to make the race—as well as any other information that it thinks important.

This can be news of great pride, as in the bulletin displayed in 1985 by March Cars Ltd., trumpeting the fact that its chassis had been on the pole for three years' running.

But sometimes the bulletin broadcasts a grimmer message, such as the one on the door of the Menard Racing garage with news of its injured driver, Herm Johnson.

Just as progress dictates constant change in race cars, so too it can dictate fundamental change in the Speedway itself (overleaf).

Despite the great pride taken in the 500's long history, in 1985 the old Garage Area had to be demolished and a new, modern Gasoline Alley built to replace it.

Gone was the fine old white ship lap construction, with its green mock-Tudor motifs.

Some of the old garages dated near the Speedway's birth. But since they'd been built for narrow cars with tall, skinny tires, they were hopelessly too tight for the low, broad racing cars of today. Alas, the need for urban renewal . . . but there are those who wonder where the ghosts of racers past, who lingered quite palpably in the shadowy corners of the old garages, waiting patiently for the running of The Great Race, will go to live now.

Construction of the new Gasoline Alley began in the summer of 1985, and the finishing touches were still being completed in May 1986. In place of the two original garage buildings, housing eighty-eight individual garage bays, the new garages are housed in three long buildings. Each new building contains thirty-two bays, for a total of ninety-six in all. Instead of running at a right angle to the pit lane, as did the old garages, the new buildings parallel it.

And in place of the old garages' flammable wood-frame construction, the new garages are built of concrete and steel.

The commodious new Garage Area (overleaf), while perhaps lacking the historic flavor of the original, is a much-improved work space.
Broad aisles between the rows of garages offer plenty of space for maneuvering.

And the garage bays themselves are considerably larger. Where the old garages were a tight 14 by 21 feet each, the new ones are a generous 20 by 25 feet, affording ample working space around the perimeters of the car. During practice days or emergency repairs, this new environment is a godsend for hard-working Indy mechanics.

In 1986, the new garages' first year, perhaps their most surprising effect was purely psychological.

With plenty of space for everyone and none of the old pressured feeling of being "packed in," the atmosphere in the remodeled Garage Area was completely changed. Intense competitive pressure will always be at Indy, yet the sheer spaciousness of the work area let everyone be just a little more easily, smile just a little more often. The old ghosts were gone, but in their place was the luxury of elbow room.

Typically, Indy-car teams are content with two garage bays, while multi-car teams may use three or four. In 1986, however, the three-car A.J. Foyt team used five garage bays. The superteam of Penske Racing contracted for no less than six garages to house its three cars—perhaps as much a matter of 'psyching-out' the opposition as of insuring adequate work room.

As the gradual job of "dialing-in" a car progresses—maximizing its power, tuning its handling and stability in Indy's terrifying high-speed turns—the Garage Area falls into a steady, workmanlike pattern. The cars are towed out to the pits for practice. Lessons are learned on the track.

Limitations are found. The cars are towed back to the garages again to be adjusted, modified, re-engineered.

A lovely softness of routine settles over the Garage Area. The power-lawnmower drone of the little tractors fills the air, as they labor faithfully day after day tugging the racers to and fro.

One by one, the cars head for the track—Al Unser Sr.'s prototype Penske PC15-Chevrolet (top row, far left) and Danny Sullivan's March 86C-Cosworth (top row, second from left). One of Sullivan's crewmen stays behind to check spare wheels

Bobby Rahal's Number 3T back-up March 86C-Cosworth sits abandoned in the Garage Area (top row, far right) while the primary car is shrieking around the Speedway, demanding the team's full attention.

In the broiling midday of a prime practice session, the Garage Area is virtually deserted. All are out at the pits, save for the few crewmen left behind to continue all-important maintenance of spare parts.

The day drones lazily on. The howl of distant racing engines fills the air, punctuated by the monotone voice of the Garage-Area paging announcer on the P.A.—he pronounces it "Grodge" Area.

The shriek of racing engines resumes, filling the void. Then one by one the cars return from the j̲_____ They're towed silently back, as if haughtily refusing to run under their own power at anything less than 200 mph.

Mario Andretti's Lola T86-Cosworth (bottom row, second from right) follows its tug, bedraped with riding crewmen. Shortly later, the March 86C-Buick of Scott Brayton (bottom row, far right) rolls back to the garages. A crewman sits on the car's sidepod, maneuvering its steering wheel.

As happens only rarely at Indianapolis, in 1986 a revolutionary new racing engine, the turbocharged Ilmor-Chevrolet V-8 (overleaf) appeared in the Garage Area. Just as in the mid-1970s the turbocharged Cosworth DFX V-8 (second overleaf, upper right, lower left and lower right) gradually supplanted the t____honored four-cylinder Meyer-Drake Offy (second overleaf, upper left), the Ilmor-Chevrolet may replace the Cosworth.

Swiss-born designer Mario Illien bends over his brainchild, warming it up in the Penske garages. Its tidy dimensions and compact fuel-injection system and intake log allow a very low, smooth engine cover at the rear of the car. Result, better streamlining, less turbulent air to the rear wing . . . and more speed.

Known as the Captain's Chair, the cockpit of an Indy car is kept absolutely as simple as possible. Yet there are critical engine functions the driver must monitor regularly. Oil and water temperature gauges warn of imminent engine failure.

Checked at certain points on the track over a number of laps, the tachometer lets the driver determine whether he is losing power or gaining speed as his fuel-load drops or a new set of tires is tried.

The manifold, or "boost," pressure gauge tells him how close his engine is coming to maximum pressure, beyond which the "pop-off" valve releases, momentarily killing power.

The gauges are rotated in their mountings so that at the optimum reading, their needles point straight up.

In current Indy cars, the tight little cockpit fits a driver like a custom-tailored suit.

Indy cars don't have self-starters. Therefore a portable electric motor like an enormous power drill is mounted to the round fitting on the back of the transmission (above).

Powerful as Indy engines are, ironically, they have very little take-off power from a standing start. The driver must slip the clutch and rev the engine, otherwise he may kill it, losing valuable time in the pits while the engine is restarted.

From the cockpit of his 1973 Eagle-Offy (right), Gordon Johncock saw every sight, that Indy has to offer. The '73 race was halted by Salt Walther's first-lap crash, then delayed two days by rain. On the third day, Swede Savage crashed. Rain shortened the race to 332.5 miles—but Johncock's last sight was the checkered flag.

Honed razor-sharp and gleaming, the four-wheeled weapon (overleaf) waits ready to qualify.

It's a New Track Record

t's six p.m. Indianapolis time on the next to last Sunday in May. For at least forty-four car and driver combinations, the Indy 500 is over. And the race hasn't even begun.

It can happen so quickly. One minute you're one of the thirty-three drivers to make the cut, the next minute you're "bumped" by someone who posted a faster time on the four-lap, ten-mile qualifying run. It's an emotional time for those who succeed and those who have to wait forty-nine agonizing weeks for another chance.

Even the strongest are reduced to tears of thankful relief when they successfully qualify. All the personal and financial risks they've taken to get to the Indy are suddenly worth it.

Failure to qualify can have the same crushing effect on veterans, fresh rookies or the guy "on the bubble"—the vulnerable driver with the slowest speed. It can destroy a driver's entire life for a year, or destroy a promising career. It means racing sprint cars on dirt-track bullrings three times a week just to meet expenses. It means working the pits and Gasoline Alley to find another car to drive. It means cancelling business commitments, speaking engagements—all plans—because on the next to last Sunday in May, you weren't up to speed.

In any other race, securing the last starting position in a field of thirty-three cars would be embarrassing. At Indianapolis, to be thirty-third is an honor, bringing the most satisfying kind of affirmation—from respected colleagues, reporters and the 200,000 or so spectators who crowd the Speedway grounds. And racing luck can be extremely rough. In 1985 Johnny Rutherford became the first three-time winner ever bumped from the starting field. Fortunately, Johnny switched to his backup machine and regained a spot on the starting grid before six p.m. on the next to last Sunday in May. Other drivers have not been so fortunate. The same year that Rutherford squeezed in, Ron Hemelgarn entered two new Lola cars, maintained by an expert team, yet neither made the starting field.

Making the field is what it's all about during "The Month," as it is called. Over the past decade, Indianapolis has attracted an average of ninety-seven entrants. That number swelled to 109 in 1982, of which 89 actually showed up in Gasoline Alley for qualifying rounds. In 1985 there wasn't enough garage space to accommodate all Indy hopefuls, so some teams were forced to set up makeshift tents outside the track, while others had to haul their machines to the track from nearby garages. But in 1986 all housing problems were resolved with the initiation of the brand-new 200,000-square-foot Gasoline Alley.

"The Month" comprises two weeks of open practice, with qualifications on the second and third weekends. It costs $3,000 to enter the race, all the more reason for making it. But on the other side of the financial equation, finishing last at Indianapolis is worth at least $75,000.

Why a field of thirty-three? The first Indy 500 in 1911 featured forty cars. The next year, the American Automobile Association, which then sanctioned auto races, decided to limit the number of starting positions for closed-course races to one car for every 400 feet of track. That ruling trimmed the field at Indianapolis to thirty-three.

The most fortunate drivers arrive at Indianapolis with team in tow, while others scour the pit areas trying to secure a high-paying ride. Each machine is allowed three attempts to qualify. The run can be aborted at any point if a team manager thinks speeds aren't fast enough, but the team can return for another attempt. And there's always the possibility—a *real* possibility—that a driver who has qualified will be bumped from the field by a faster driver, who had himself been bumped in another car the day before. It's that fickle.

The fastest car-driver combination on the first day of time trials wins the opportunity to start the race at the front of the field on the pole—specifically, on the inside, next to two other drivers. This vantage point gives him a wide open track when the green starter's flag drops. If qualifying thirty-third on the grid is a victory in itself, then winning the pole position is just icing on the victory cake. There's a cash bonus for the pole driver. Pancho Carter won an extra $75,000 in prizes and gifts for his record-breaking pole run in 1985, and Rick Mears earned over $100,000 in 1986. But there's something more to winning the pole at Indianapolis than an enviable starting position and prize money. It's a tradition that carries an honor unparalleled in any other race.

To reach the pole position, a driver must perform faster and better than anyone else. It's a great feeling to announce to the crowd, "It's a new track record," and see them stand and cheer in approval. These exciting moments are remembered long after the fans are gone.

High speeds and track records are as big a part of the Indy 500 as taking the Victory Lap. Spectators have come to expect it. Drivers push for it. And officials of the United States Auto Club, the organization that supervises and sanctions the race, voice a genuine concern when qualifying speeds exceed 210 mph. Each season they modify construction rules in hope of slowing down the machines. Car designers and mechanics, however, take those new rules and ingeniously design a race car that goes even faster. There's been a new track record set at Indianapolis every year since 1981. Ironically, the men who fine-tune the machines, making new records possible—the mechanics and engineers—are quickly forgotten by the fans. Their attention is focused on the driver and his machine.

Tom Sneva: The Speed King

Since 1977 Tom Sneva has become known as Indianapolis's speed hero. Just to call Tom's departure from the starting line on a qualification run starts the fans roaring. Over the years, they've learned that Sneva's a tough competitor, and his colleagues agree. He's fast and he's strong. When the five-foot, eleven-inch dynamo straps himself into the cockpit, he's ready to charge the course.

Tom became the first driver to break the 200-mph barrier in that 1977 run for the pole. With a speed of 200.535 mph on his initial lap, Tom became an overnight hero. He's sat on the pole three times since 1977. On each occasion, he set a new track record. He was the fastest rookie qualifier in 1974, and he's been the man to beat ever since.

Tom's background didn't exactly prepare him for a career in car racing. A graduate of Eastern Washington State College, Tom became a teacher, coach and then principal of a small school in Washington state. Tom earned a modest $6,700 annual salary, and another $225 a year for coaching basketball and football. In May 1973, Tom convinced the school board to give him a leave of absence so he could take the rookie test at Indianapolis. But apparently the school board wasn't pleased by Tom's endeavor. The board gave him an ultimatum: Teach school or quit. "It took me probably thirty seconds to decide which way I wanted to go," Tom recalls. "I had a wife and two children and some security in the educational field. But we decided to go racing."

Driving a chassis manufactured by Grant King in his own shop near the Speedway, Tom qualified for Indy in 1974. His performance in subsequent championship races prompted owner Roger Penske to select Tom for the 1975 Indy 500.

Sneva's career with Penske had a notable beginning. Driving the Norton Spirit, Tom started fourth and was moving well into the second turn when he clipped the left front wheel of another car. He hit the wall hard in front of the high-priced executive suites, sending spectators scurrying from the verandas to dodge the flying debris. It was one of the most spectacular accidents in Speedway history. The engine and accompanying rear suspension ripped away from the machine as it flipped. The car landed upright with Tom pinned in what was left of the tub. Within seconds, fire crews had the fire out, and Sneva, still conscious, was dragged from the

wreck and placed in an ambulance.

Sneva's crash received tremendous publicity, partly because the ABC television cameras were on the turn at the time of the accident. "You see so many accidents happen on a test day when there's no one around," Tom later remarked. "And the driver might get hurt a lot worse than I did, but their accidents don't get the coverage. Looking back on it now, it probably didn't hurt my career to have that exposure."

Leave it to Tom to crash in front of the $30,000 suites instead of in front of the fifteen-dollar seats along the back stretch. Tom's strong-willed personality and undeniable charisma make him a real showman. I remember an interview with him the night before the pole run in 1977. We were discussing which driver would post the top speed during qualifying. I suggested A. J. Foyt or Al or Bobby Unser. "Wait a minute," Tom interrupted, "you're talking to the driver who's going to be on the pole."

Sure enough, Sneva set a new track record the next day with a blazing average speed of 198.884. Sneva dueled with A. J. Foyt throughout the race, and the two finished on the same lap. Foyt won the event by thirty seconds. For his effort, Tom earned $100,000 more than his annual salary as a schoolteacher just four short years before.

It's a New Track Record

Driving for the Penske team in 1978, Tom once again demonstrated his superb skills as a driver to the delight of the thousands of spectators who packed the stands for the time trials. Starter Pat Vidan waved the green flag to Sneva. Tom drove a perfect groove in all four turns. "It's a new track record. Time for the first lap, 44.20 seconds. Speed average, 203.620 mph."

Sneva's Norton Spirit recorded three more laps over the magic 200 mph mark, and then the time and speed report for the total run was compiled. "It's another new track record," I screamed into the microphone. "Total time for the ten-mile run,

2:58:008. Speed average, 202.156 mph." The crowd cheered as Sneva slowed and headed for the check-in area at the south end of the pits. The fans had just witnessed the first 200-mph qualifying run at Indianapolis.

Sneva, Danny Ongais and Rick Mears all averaged over 200 mph to form the front row for race day. For the second time, Sneva finished second, 9.9 seconds behind Al Unser.

Sneva parted company with Penske Racing after the 1978 season, and it was several years before he got the support of another major team. However, he did finish second in the race in 1980. In that event, Tom crashed in practice prior to the race. Like most top-flight race drivers, Sneva arrived at Indy with a backup machine, which guaranteed his starting position. But the rules required that he start in thirty-third position. This was only a slight inconvenience to Tom. His experience on the oval course enabled him to charge all the way to another second place, finishing a half-lap behind the yellow Chaparral of Johnny Rutherford.

Reflecting on his successful years with Penske Racing, Tom says with the greatest sincerity, "I didn't know how efficient they were until I left."

Sneva joined a new team, Bignotti-Cotter Racing in 1982. With this new crew Tom dominated Indianapolis a year later, although his speed records were successfully challenged by rookie Teo Fabi, placing Tom in the fourth starting position. A native Italian and Grand Prix veteran, Fabi shocked the racing fraternity by qualifying with a 207.395 mph average in the Skoal Bandit.

Memorable Moments

At least one controversy takes place at each race, and the 1983 season's challenge involved Sneva and the Unser father-son combination. Driving for Roger Penske, Al Sr. had the lead but was being pursued relentlessly by Sneva. Running close together, Unser and Sneva were separated by Al Unser Jr., who was several laps behind and not in

Year	Driver	Chassis	mph
1911	Lewis Strang	Case	over 75.00
1912	Gil Anderson	Stutz	80.93
1913	Caleb Bragg	Mercer	87.34
1914	Jean Chassagne	Sunbeam	88.31
1915	Howard Wilcox	Stutz	98.90
1916	John Aitken	Peugeot	96.69
1919	Rene Thomas	Ballot	104.78
1920	Ralph DePalma	Ballot	99.15
1921	Ralph DePalma	Ballot	100.75
1922	Jimmy Murphy	Duesenberg	100.50
1923	Tommy Milton	Miller	108.17
1924	Jimmy Murphy	Miller	108.037
1925	Leon Duray	Miller	113.196
1926	Earl Cooper	Miller	111.735
1927	Frank Lockhart	Miller	120.100
1928	Leon Duray	Miller	122.391
1929	Cliff Woodbury	Miller	120.599
1930	Billy Arnold	Summers	113.268
1931	Russ Snowberger	Snowberger	112.796
1932	Lou Moore	Miller	117.363
1933	Bill Cummings	Miller	118.530
1934	Kelly Petillo	Adams	119.329
1935	Rex Mays	Adams	120.736
1936	Rex Mays	Adams	119.644
1937	Bill Cummings	Miller	123.343
1938	Floyd Roberts	Wetteroth	125.681
1939	Jimmy Snyder	Adams	130.138
1940	Rex Mays	Stevens	127.850
1941	Mauri Rose	Maserati	128.691
1946	Cliff Bergere	Wetteroth	126.471
1947	Ted Horn	Maserati	126.564
1948	Rex Mays	Kurtis	130.577
1949	Duke Nalon	Kurtis	132.939
1950	Walt Faulkner	KK2000	134.343
1951	Duke Nalon	Kurtis	136.498

Pole Winners

Year	Driver	Chassis	mph
1952	Fred Agabashian	Kurtis	138.010
1953	Bill Vukovich	KK500A	138.392
1954	Jack McGrath	KK500C	141.033
1955	Jerry Hoyt	Stevens	140.045
1956	Pat Flaherty	Watson	145.596
1957	Pat O'Connor	KK500G	143.948
1958	Dick Rathmann	Watson	145.974
1959	Johnny Thomson	Lesovsky	145.908
1960	Eddie Sachs	Ewing	146.592
1961	Eddie Sachs	Ewing	147.481
1962	Parnelli Jones	Watson	150.370
1963	Parnelli Jones	Watson	151.153
1964	Jim Clark	Lotus	158.828
1965	A. J. Foyt	Lotus	161.233
1966	Mario Andretti	Brawner	165.899
1967	Mario Andretti	Hawk	168.982
1968	Joe Leonard	Lotus	171.559
1969	A. J. Foyt	Coyote	170.568
1970	Al Unser	P. J. Colt	170.221
1971	Peter Revson	McLaren	178.696
1972	Bobby Unser	Eagle	195.940
1973	J. Rutherford	McLaren	198.413
1974	A. J. Foyt	Coyote	191.632
1975	A. J. Foyt	Coyote	193.976
1976	J. Rutherford	McLaren	188.957
1977	Tom Sneva	McLaren	198.884
1978	Tom Sneva	Penske	202.156
1979	Rick Mears	Penske	193.736
1980	J. Rutherford	Chaparral	192.256
1981	Bobby Unser	Penske PC-9B	200.546
1982	Rick Mears	Penske PC-10	207.004
1983	Teo Fabi	March	207.395
1984	Tom Sneva	March	210.029
1985	Pancho Carter	March	212.583
1986	Rick Mears	March	216.828

contention for the lead. Each time Sneva tried to pass Little Al, the rookie would shift three or four feet to the left on the straight, thereby "shutting the door" on the charging Sneva. Young Unser's actions, while disturbing to some fans and reporters, were totally legal; he was merely creating an annoyance for Sneva. Finally, on lap 191, Sneva maneuvered his way through traffic, got around both Unsers, and went on to his first Indy victory. Sneva's decisive ten-second lead over Al Unser Sr. earned him nearly $400,000. It was a sweet victory for the man who has given the Speedway many exciting moments.

Sneva's finest performance in qualifications was yet to come. Pole day, May 12, 1984. As usual, the drivers drew for qualifying order the night before. Sometimes the luck of the draw makes for an exciting speed show. This year was no exception. Rick Mears, driving the Number 6 Pennzoil, took the first lap at 208.502 mph. "It's a new track record," I roared from the start-finish line. Mears's subsequent three laps were slower, squashing his attempt to break the four-lap speed average of Teo Fabi. But at least Mears was the proud owner of the new single-lap record.

Mario Andretti was next out. Mario took the first lap at a blazing 209.678 mph—another new track record. Mario's times for the next two laps in the Number 3 Budweiser Lola were down slightly, but Mario still looked to be on his way to a new ten-mile record. As luck would have it, the Lola's electrical system malfunctioned at the fourth turn of the final lap, slowing the car to just over 202 mph. Fabi's record was still safe.

"Tom Terrific" was next in line. As Tom's Texaco Star left the starting line, the fans cheered in anticipation of a spectacular, record-breaking run. Sneva's first lap, 209.113 mph, was just a tick under Andretti's record. But he bettered the time on the second lap, giving the Speed King yet another new track record. By now the crowd was on its feet. Sneva took his third lap at 210.423 mph. "It's the first 210-mph lap in Speedway history. Another new

track record!" I exclaimed, only to repeat myself less than a minute later when Sneva completed his fourth lap in 42.717 seconds at 210.689 mph. What a showman. Total time for his run was 2:51:405, at an average speed of 210.029 mph. It's rare for a driver to do each lap faster, but then, Tom's a rare and talented sportsman. In a span of just over two hours, spectators had witnessed the Speedway's finest speed pursuit ever. The records had tumbled six times! Indianapolis records are destined to fall. And Sneva's marks, however spectacular, were destined to hold for but a single year.

The Buick V-6 racing engine enabled Scott Brayton and Pancho Carter to steal Sneva's records in 1985. Brayton, a native of Coldwater, Michigan, set new single-lap records on his first three laps. But he experienced mechanical problems on the final lap, which jeopardized his overall average speed. Pancho Carter won the pole position and set a new speed record of 212.583 mph.

In 1986 speed records pushed even higher. "Oh, no! You won't believe it! It's over 217 mph!" Rick Mears had set a new one-lap record, four miles an hour faster than Carter's record of just one year ago. Mears's fastest lap was 217.581; his four-lap average of 216.828 earned him a third start from the pole.

Making History

With speeds of over 210 mph becoming the norm, it's sometimes easy to forget that the early Indy races went at a much slower pace. The first driver to break the 100-mph mark was Ralph DePalma, driving a Ballot in 1921. Eighteen years later, Louis Meyer became the first to qualify over 125 mph, posting a qualifying time of 130.067 mph. In the early 1960s, drivers raced to break the 150-mph mark. It finally happened in 1962—the first time the two-and-one-half mile course was completed in less than a minute. Driving for car owner J. C. Agajanian, Parnelli Jones ran one lap at 150.729, and his total run averaged 150.370 mph. When Parnelli broke the barrier, there was a wild celebration at the starting line, led by Agajanian

wearing his familiar cowboy hat.

A Brown University engineering graduate, Mark Donohue was the first to break the 175-mph mark. Driving for Penske Racing, Mark hit 177.087 in 1971, only to be beaten for the pole position by Peter Revson, who clocked in at a record 178.696 mph.

Is there no limit to the speeds? Probably not. As long as drivers compete, there are no limits to progress at the Indy 500.

Persistence Pays Off

Johnny Rutherford was the first to flirt with the 200-mph lap mark in the early 1970s. Rutherford's career is a case study of the will to succeed. Johnny is one of the few drivers who has persevered through tough times and gone on to capture racing's biggest prize—not once but three times. The Texas gentleman finally captured the Indy 500 title after ten attempts.

Johnny's been racing for more than twenty years, and he's one of few drivers who successfully made the switch from sprint-car competition to Indy cars. Sprint-car drivers generally don't excel on the circuit because they're not experienced with road racing or rear-engine machines. Rutherford suffered his share of misfortunes early in his career. In Eldora, Ohio, in 1966 Rutherford's car flipped over the outside guardrail, leaving him with two broken arms and keeping him off the circuit for a year. During one of his early visits to Methodist Hospital in Indianapolis, he met a nurse, who would later become Mrs. Betty Rutherford.

Johnny's first Indianapolis victory finally came in 1974. Driving for England's Team McLaren in the twenty-fifth starting position, Rutherford led for 122 laps to earn his first Indy title. His second victory came two years later. Johnny had the lead at the half-way point when it started to rain. Three laps later, the race was red-flagged. After a two-hour delay, the race was officially called, and Betty and Johnny walked to Victory Lane for the ceremony. "I'm proud and happy to win, but I would

have liked to race for it," Johnny quipped. You can say a lot of things about Johnny Rutherford—all positive. Congenial with the media, a superb public speaker, no driver has been a better salesman for the 500 than Johnny.

In 1980 Rutherford became a three-time winner. And this time he did have to "race for it." Johnny took the checkered flag in Jim Hall's Pennzoil Chaparral with three other drivers close behind—Sneva, Gary Bettenhausen and Gordon Johncock. Johnny was so excited about his third Indianapolis victory that, on his final cool-down lap, he stopped beside Tim Richmond's car, which had run out of fuel with only half a straightaway to go. Rutherford offered Tim a ride and motored into Victory Lane, the first winner ever to give a lift to another driver. After ten long years of disappointments, Rutherford had set a new track record, won the pole position three times, and captured his third Indy title—all within the short span of eight years.

Jigger Jinx

Even the most persistent drivers can't always make it. Back in 1969—before the rules guaranteed a pole shot to all cars waiting in line on the first day—rain washed out all but one attempt on Day One of qualifying. Rookie Jigger Sirois took three laps at speeds averaging over 161 mph. But his crew decided it wasn't fast enough and called him in. Then the rains returned, and as it turned out, no one else tried to qualify that day.

If not for his crew, Jigger would have won the pole position and qualified for his first race. In later attempts, he failed to make the field, and in fact, after two more tries in subsequent years, Jigger was through as a Speedway hopeful. An error in judgment had robbed him of a pole position, as well as a chance to run.

Each year, the American Auto Racing Writers and Broadcasters gives an award to the driver suffering the worst luck during qualifying. It's the Jigger Award, presented in the name of the man who had the pole secured and lost it.

Anticipation

Drivers tell me that, during qualifications, I am the personification of the voice of fate. As the track's announcer, it's my duty to inform the spectators of each contestant's speed. Before a driver rolls down the pit road to qualify, he knows to the hundredth of a mile per hour the speed he needs to make the starting grid. But there is no odometer on the instrument panel to indicate speed—the dial only shows rpm's. Really, there's no chance to drive by instruments anyway. It's the feel of the machine that translates speed to the driver, as well as his own fine-tuned "qualifying" metabolism.
During the run, engine noise and the high speeds keep drivers from hearing the public address announcements. And although pit crews indicate unofficial speeds each lap on a pit board as the driver roars out of the fourth turn, the drivers say, once off the course and out of the car, that they await my confirmation of their official speed with the same helpless, intense anticipation as a prospective army draftee or an expectant father. One of the greatest pleasures of working the microphone at Indianapolis is to be able to tell a driver—the guy "on the bubble"—that his dream is real.

The moment to qualify is here. No turning back. Either everything goes perfectly and the car "makes the show" . . . or else what? There is no other alternative, really. The car must make the show. Since the previous Indy 500, a year's worth of finding sponsorship, assembling a team, buying a car and arranging all the equipment necessary to support it have all been directed at making a success of this one moment—the qualifying run.

The tension is blinding. Normally calm, easy-going drivers become cold, fragile. Their eyes go narrow, darting about. Their lips are pursed.

Small mistakes and delays suddenly seem enormous obstacles that only a miracle can remove. But one by one, each obstacle is overcome. The qualifying line creeps slowly, agonizingly forward.

Time is either racing ahead, or standing perfectly stationary— it's impossible to know which. All movement, all activity, takes place out of the context of time, for this is a process with its own momentum. Once caught up in it, the participants are carried helplessly along.

Yet they draw ever nearer to the chilling moment when, all inspections and briefings completed, the driver is strapped tight to his car. For the first time in deadly earnest, the mighty 800-horsepower racing engine behind him comes to roaring life.

From that moment on, he is entirely alone with the track. He must go exactly as fast as his car and engine and tires—and the brutal, unforgiving concrete wall—will allow. To go any slower risks dropping him from the race. To go any faster risks consequences darker still. For the next several minutes, success or failure rests entirely upon his skill, judgment, courage, luck—and fate.

QUALIFYING ORDER & SPEED
AS DRAWN

No.	DRIVER	SPEED	No.	DRIVER	SPEED
23	SIMON	1ST A.	25	ONGAIS	209.158
2	ANDRETTI SR.	212.300	15	CARTER	209.635
21	RUTHERFORD	1ST A.	16	T. BETTENHAUSEN	208.933
61	LUYENDYK	1ST A.	33	SNEVA	211.878
1	SULLIVAN	215.382	66	PIMM	210.874
59	GANASSI	1ST A.	61	LUYENDYK	2ND A.
33T	SNEVA	1ST A.			
12	LANIER	209.964			
4	MEARS	216.828			
20	FITTIPALDI	210.237			
8	BRABHAM	1ST A.			
18T	ANDRETTI, JR.	214.522			
81T	VILLENEUVE	209.397			
9	MORENO	209.469			
3T	RAHAL	213.550			
66	PIMM	1ST A.			
30T	UNSER, JR.	211.533			
36	FIRESTONE	1ST A.			
55	GARZA	208.939			
7	COGAN	211.922			

The first day of qualifying.
High-noon at Indy.

Despite the fact that hot sun
will broil the track surface,
overheat the tires and rob the
engine of horsepower, most
front-runners are eager to
take their place in line on
this first day. The rules state
that unless a car that
qualifies on the first day is
not among the thirty-three
fastest-qualifiers, whatever
grid position it achieves that
day will be its position on
race day.

In fact, even if on a later day
a car qualifies faster than the
pole winner—this has
happened—the faster car
must start the race behind
the slowest first-day
qualifier. To qualify on the
first day, then, whether in
blazing sun or not,
guarantees a good place on
the starting grid.

As the qualifying order
creeps ahead (left), the teams
prod at their cars. The drivers
hide under sun umbrellas,
trying to stay cool.

USAC officials give each car a
full technical inspection.

The cars' sidepods are tested
to be certain that they don't
"accidentally" sag at top
speed, giving the car an
unfair advantage in greater
cornering downforce as it
goes through the turns. Wing
heights and dimensions,
underbody height and vehicle
weight are also checked.

When a car has satisfied the
scrutineers, it is pushed to
the front of the line.

The moment is near
(overleaf). Steering wheel
removed for ease of entry,
Gary Bettenhausen of the
popular Bettenhausen clan,
climbs into his March-
Cosworth to qualify. His
lame left arm, severely
injured in a racing accident
years before, hangs limp.

His helmet is supported by a
thickly cushioned collar,
holding it upright against
the vicious g-forces generated
in the turns at Indy.

For the few, qualifying at Indy is not a question of "if," so much as "how well."

Acknowledged masters of the Speedway like Rick Mears (left) and the brilliant young Michael Andretti (below), both seen in 1986, engage in a fierce duel of maximum speed during qualifying. The prize is the glamour and prestige of starting from the pole.

In view of the fact that in seventy-one Indy 500s only twelve pole-sitters have won the race, the honor of starting from the pole may seem somewhat hollow. Yet Indy remains a deeply ceremonial auto race and, short of winning the 500 itself, no single achievement is more greatly honored than to be the car that leads all others to the green flag on race day.

Before going onto the track to qualify (overleaf), each driver receives a careful briefing from chief steward Tom Binford. The driver will be allowed a warm-up lap, then the green flag is dropped and the four-lap qualifying attempt begins. If the team feels the car is going too slowly to make the field, it may "wave off" the attempt. However, each car is strictly

PROVIMI
VEAL
SIMPSON
ROVIMI
61
Dutch
Treats
SPORT
MAGAZINE

More and more, the driver
becomes a solitary figure,
bound to his car. Whether
he's four-time winner A.J.
Foyt (above), racing at the
Speedway for four decades,
or Scott Brayton (right),
preparing in 1986 to qualify
for his fifth 500, the racetrack
is the same chilly wilderness.
Despite the multitudes in the
stands, he is now alone,
totally separate. Imprisoned
in the narrow confines of the
cockpit, he must clear his
mind of all but the pavement
ahead.

The starter motor is inserted
at the back of the car. It
whines. The engine coughs.
One by one, the cylinders
catch. The driver nurses it
with the throttle. Suddenly,
in a raucous fanfare of
horsepower, it rages to life.

Last-minute reminders, bits
of counsel and
encouragement, are offered
by the crew . . . but already
they are irrelevant. The
outside world is a void. Only
the driver exists.

With painful tooth-by-tooth grinding, the straight-cut, non-synchromesh gearbox finds first gear. The engine races.

The driver (Tom Sneva in 1986, left) spins the clutch. The car inches ahead. Very slowly at first, it gains momentum. The engine is balky, wanting either to stop completely or shriek off at full power.

But the driver must be very gentle with it now, care for it —warm it gradually for one complete lap, insuring that its running heat has soaked through every one of its thousands of finely polished surfaces. Only then, with all its internal stresses resolved, will it survive the strain of generating sustained maximum horsepower for ten miles straight.

The ranks of crewmen who have followed the car through the qualifying line, bending over it, peering at it, wiping and polishing, making certain all is as it must be . . . fade into the distance behind.

Only the team's timers, who must decide whether to accept the speed of this run, or wave-off and try for greater speed later, are of material help now.

Tensely, they wait for the car to appear coming out of Turn Four. On the earphones they listen for any indication from the driver that there is trouble. In moments, he will appear . . .

INDIANAPOLIS

500

MAY 25, 1986

Starter Duane Sweeney
(above) holds out the
stationary yellow flag during
the car's warm-up lap.

Then, going into Turn One,
its engine note begins to
climb. From the pits you
hear it on the backstraight,
climbing and climbing

The qualifying car, this masterpiece of engineering, is suddenly reduced to four narrow patches of black rubber on flat pavement. For just under three minutes, the driver must devote every atom of his energy to keeping those four patches streaking down the straightaways, clawing through the turns.

There is a flash of bright color in the distance. Streaking sidelong, coming desperately close to the outside wall in Turn Four, engine screaming, it shrieks towards the starter's green flag.

He's on it!

Four laps. Ten miles.

One of the best at this in 1986 was Michael Andretti (above). He qualified at 214.522 mph, good enough for the outside of the front row.

As suddenly as it begins, it's over. The huge crowd in the stands roars its approval as the last car to qualify comes off the track. To save wear on the delicate racing engine, it's already shut off.

Now this violent object, only moments before a howling banshee, rolls silently down the bumpy concrete slabs of the pit lane. The fat racing tires make a low rumble as it passes by.

It veers left into the post-qualification photo enclosure. Once again, the crew crowds around, as the driver releases his safety harness.

He emerges at last, undoing his helmet, and the first to greet him is his wife. Betty Rutherford (left) gives husband Johnny a big kiss after he has qualified in 1986.

But the scene after qualifying is not always one of joy and hosannas. Only the thirty-three fastest cars will make the field, yet there are always more than thirty-three cars trying to qualify. And as the field begins to fill, slower cars are in danger of being "bumped" off the grid by late qualifiers with higher speeds.

Tony Bettenhausen had to sweat it out in 1985 (above). After early engine problems, he didn't qualify until the second weekend—and even then, it wasn't clear that his speed of 204.824 mph would be fast enough. In the end, though, his challengers all failed and he got the victor's kiss from wife Shirley.

He'd made the show.

Financing the Dream

Money spins the wheels of commerce and money spins the roulette wheels at Monte Carlo. It is almost equal measures of money, business acumen and blind luck that power the wheels of major-league racing.

For new drivers hoping to break into the circuit, it usually takes years of a commitment approaching religious fervor to find the funds needed—perhaps two million dollars—to race for a single season. Without determination, the driver won't last long enough to find the dollars. But even with the devotion of a fanatic and the backing of a well-heeled sponsor, no driver can anticipate how a simple twist of fate may derail his career. An engine failure can end the season before it begins. A spin-out and crash in practice can finish a good run before the first Indy-car race.

The cash that fuels the race circuit comes from a complex mix of sources. Money from the sale of broadcast rights and tickets is distributed to teams through USAC and CART in the form of prizes and guarantees. Racing teams may have a few very wealthy owners who can afford the long-shot odds and multimillion dollar risk of fielding a car or they may be backed by a patchwork of numerous, less affluent investors. Then there are corporate sponsors, companies that bet that putting their names on the side of a race car will help sell their products. Keeping revenue streams flowing smoothly is a juggling act that takes valuable time away from engineering and driving—the two things that actually win races. But without the money, there's no race to win.

Two drivers, still at the beginning of their careers, are now fighting this battle of dollars versus determination. The recent experiences of Tony Bettenhausen Jr. and Derek Daly, teammates just two years ago, are typical.

A Short Success Story

In 1981 the future of driver Tony Bettenhausen Jr. looked promising. Although he was a rookie at Indianapolis, the sharp, solidly built thirty-one year old was already a twelve-year veteran of USAC racing in midget and sprint cars, long the accepted training ground for Speedway drivers until the advent of rear-engine machines and road courses. In 1972 Tony was runner-up in the NASCAR late-model sportsman standings. He was born to the track. His father, the late Tony Bettenhausen Sr., was a two-time national champion in the 1950s who died in a crash while testing a car at Indianapolis in 1961. Tony Jr.'s older brother, Gary, a solid competitor with fifteen Indy starts to his credit, was often a source of valuable advice.

A decade on the track is a career for some drivers. After this experience, Tony's backers were ready for the pinnacle of major-league racing—a start at Indy. They purchased a year-old McClaren chassis, complete with motor, for $60,000. Tony made the field at the Speedway, finishing seventh. He went on to take second at the Michigan 500 and finished sixth in the 1981 CART National Championship standings, ahead of such stalwarts as Bobby and Al Unser, Tom Sneva and Mario Andretti.

Even with all of his experience, Tony was an oval-track driver, but the seventeen race Indy-car circuit also includes road-race courses. Bettenhausen attended two driving schools to sharpen his road-race skills; by 1983 he was quick enough on the challenging over-the-road courses to qualify eleventh and sit alongside veteran Rick Mears at Laguna Seca. Running fifth, with just twenty laps to go, the engine blew. Still, Tony considers that his best run on a road course, and the next year brought an offer from the Provimi Racing team. He and driver Derek Daly signed on to pilot the well-equipped team's two new March cars.

Early in the season, Daly qualified second fastest at Long Beach in a machine that had been meticulously prepared. Tony's car, however, had arrived late and there was no chance to test it thoroughly. "It wouldn't shift," Tony recalls. "It would shift in the pits, but when the engine heated up, the heads expanded and they put a bind in the shifting linkage. We had the wrong ring and pinion in and we missed the race." Tony hasn't run a road course since. Provimi fired him.

Despite this rebuff from an established team, Tony has put together his own Indianapolis effort. His supporters are "friends and neighbors," he says, none of them wealthy enough to field a team alone, but eager to participate in Tony's pursuit of the dream. This loyal group put him in the 1985 starting field at Indianapolis. Two days of qualifying had already passed when Tony got the opportunity to buy Tom Sneva's back-up machine, a Lola. Despite a lack of practice and very limited technical assistance, Tony got the Lola qualified. But a faulty wheel bearing put him out of the race on the thirty-first lap.

Without the money to compete in the events remaining on the schedule, the Lola was sold back to the Dan Gurney team to replace the car Sneva crashed in the race. Tony's investors got their money back, but he was sidelined for the rest of the season. The man who had qualified at Indianapolis four consecutive years was without a job. For Tony, no racing meant no income, and he had a wife and daughter to support, so he became an automobile salesman.

The same group of supporters backed Tony again in 1986. The investors put out $140,000 for a new March 86-C chassis, and Tony found two used Cosworth engines. Right up until race time, Bettenhausen had no idea whether he'd be able to raise the cash needed to pay a chief mechanic and crew. As he put it, "It's definitely a shoestring operation. But I had faith that, once the machine arrived at Gasoline Alley, somehow we'd run it."

That faith paid off. Tony qualified in the middle of the pack with a solid 209 mph. For finishing twenty-eighth, Tony earned $77,712.50 in prize money, but the amount was nowhere near enough to cover the expense of the Indy race or to enable him to compete full-time on the championship trail. Tony's only means of paying for his 1986 investment was to put the new March up for sale and hope for a buyer.

Luck of the Irish?

Tony's teammate on the 1981 Provimi team was Derek Daly. One look at the man and you know he's Irish. Born in Dublin, Derek has an engaging smile and sense of humor that have already assured him a move from the track to the broadcast booth whenever he's ready. His rich Irish brogue is filled with colorful expressions, compressing great events into a few well-chosen words. When Derek was twelve years old, his father took him to see a road race at Donboyne, Ireland. The experience gripped him, and he was determined to become a race driver. At sixteen, he started a three-year "saloon" racing career. Saloon racing is the equivalent of a demolition derby in the U.S., the winner being the last car left on the track. In 1972 he won the Irish national saloon-racing title.

Derek began "proper road racing," as he calls it, two years later. To finance the venture, he borrowed almost $1,500 from a bank on the pretext of starting his own auto sales business. Instead, he bought a Formula Ford and went racing. At the end of the year, he still owed the bank $1,500. With Ireland's economy on the ropes, that was a considerable sum to an unemployed race driver. Derek heard of a job in the iron-ore mines in Australia. Anyone who was willing, and had the strength, could work day and night. He spent the winter in Australia, returning six months later with enough money to pay off the loan, purchase a new Formula Ford and go racing again. Daly won the Irish championship that year—and he was on his way to the big time.

For the 1976 season, Derek bought a bus, took all of

the seats out, and put his race car in the back and a bed in the front. He lived like a gypsy, racing the circuit in England that year. After winning twenty-three Formula Ford races, he moved up to Formula Three, won the British championship in 1977, then finished third in the European Formula Two series the following year.

Success followed success as Daly drove in Grand Prix competition for four teams—Tyrell, March, Theodore and Williams. Soon, he was ready for a new challenge. He tried American oval racing, debuting at Phoenix in 1982, and liked it. The Indianapolis race was next, and he qualified for the 500 in 1983.

The Irishman's skill did not go unnoticed: In 1984 he was signed to drive for Team Provimi. Daly's stint in the Australian mines must have seemed far behind him now; a ride with a major-league American racing team is a long way from the Irish saloon-racing circuit. But, just as it did for teammate Tony Bettenhausen Jr., fate intervened. During the Michigan 200-miler late in the season, Derek's car went out of control and his leg was shattered.

In a few short seconds, Daly's career as a driver was over. Many observers on the circuit questioned whether he would ever walk again, much less drive an Indy car in competition. But Daly went to Methodist Hospital in Indianapolis. Orthopedic surgeon Dr. Terry Trammel is an expert in the repair of injuries caused by high-speed impact. He took a bone from Derek's hip, rebuilt the lower half of one leg, and created a new ankle joint.

While Dr. Trammel was able to put Derek's body back together, it would take longer to repair the damage to his career. Without a ride for 1985 and with the racing fraternity dubious about his health, Daly went to the season's first race at Long Beach, California, to be seen. He met a man who wanted to be a car owner and, as Derek says, "talked faster than I could listen, always in the millions of dollars." Daly quickly whipped a team together for the 1985 Indy 500, but the sponsor's pockets weren't quite

deep enough. While he had a chassis, Derek had no engine. Desperate, with time running out, Daly found his answer in a bar on Thirty-eighth Street in Indianapolis. There on display, he discovered a 1982 Eagle with the engine he needed. He bought the engine, and miraculously qualified and finished twelfth in the race.

The luck of the Irish would only take the fiercely determined driver so far, however. There was no more money. His car repossessed, Daly faced the remainder of the season without a ride, but not without employment. He provided the expert commentary for several cable-television race broadcasts. While his performance on camera is as solid as his accomplishments on the oval, Daly's immediate interest is racing, not television broadcasting.

Although Provimi again signed Daly for the 1986 Indy race, shortly after the month started, this sponsor decided against running a second machine for Daly. Eventually, he was hired by the Menard team to replace Herm Johnson, who had wrecked early in the month. Driving the rebuilt machine, Daly was on his second lap of the final day of qualifying when rain washed out his run and ended his bid for a fourth consecutive start.

Money Matters

Like dozens of their contemporaries, Bettenhausen and Daly continue to struggle with the vagaries of finding backers, competing with marginal equipment and staying healthy. Their sights are set on joining racing's elite—the small group of drivers who are guaranteed a ride season after season, who have well-financed, ambitious owners, skilled crews, first-class equipment and an annual retainer of $200,000 or more.

Tom Sneva, Al Unser Sr., Rick Mears, Danny Sullivan, Geoff Brabham, Emerson Fittipaldi, Al Unser Jr., Bob Rahal and Roberto Moreno are among this aristocracy. Mario Andretti reportedly has a guarantee of one million dollars a year. In addition, the driver receives forty percent of all

purses won by the car. This driver's share is a long-standing tradition that originated in racing's early days, when drivers' careers were often cut short by serious injury or even death. Today, however, racing is far safer, and some team owners have successfully revised their driver's share of the purse downward, perhaps as low as twenty-five percent. Still, most get the full forty percent, and winning Indianapolis can make the driver $200,000 richer in one stroke.

Moreover, winning at Indianapolis can mean the chance to earn an additional one million dollars through advertising endorsements, speeches and public appearances. Tom Sneva and Bob Hope promote Texaco products on television, Johnny Rutherford has endorsed Volkswagen cars, A.J. Foyt is pictured alongside a Houston freeway talking about Valvoline, and Dan Gurney does most of his public driving for Toyota.

The Andretti clan is an exceptional case. The automobile products company STP has signed Mario and his sons, Michael and Jeff, to a series of contracts. Mario and Michael are racing Indy cars, while Jeff is mastering the art of driving in the Super Vee series.

As guarantees to top drivers have soared, so have the salaries of other members of the team. In 1985 annual salaries for a chief mechanic and engineer averaged $60,000, while mechanics averaged $25,000 to $40,000. The crew also shares in prizes, with ten percent of purses won being distributed among the crew members. The chief mechanic usually gets the largest share.

Long Way to the Bottom Line

The establishment driver or mechanic can make an excellent living out of the race circuit. But there's an old saying: "Speed costs money. How fast do you want to go?" The costs to the owner of a team or to the backer of an individual driver are staggering. According to Dennis Hardy and Phil Casey of Cotter Racing, it costs better than a million and a half just to get to the table. The next step is to hire

a driver, chief mechanic and crew, and engineer, rent a headquarters, install a telephone, and you're off to the races—and in line to pay more bills. Race-track testing costs an average of $10,000 a day. Moving the car and crew around, housing and feeding them averages $120,000 annually. Tires, supplied below their manufacturing cost by Goodyear, still run between $40,000 and $50,000 for a season.

Owners have to expect that one or more of their machines will be wiped out in accidents. Rick Galles lost two in one race at Michigan in 1984. At better than $150,000 per car, a serious crash can wipe out the team's budget in a few tenths of a second. It is possible to insure cars, but the premiums are very high. Lloyd's of London has insured cars competing at Indianapolis, but the premium is $20,000 minimum—so teams that can afford to buy another chassis and rebuild usually take their chances. Owner Lee Brayton insured driver Patrick Bedard's entry in the 1984 Indianapolis 500. The car disintegrated when it flipped end over end during the fifty-fifth lap, so Brayton's investment was a wise one.

Payday

The team owner can only hope that a car crosses the finish line enough times to defray its purchase price before being destroyed or becoming obsolete. The money won by finishing or winning races can help owners recoup some of their expenses. In 1985 two events were added on the Indy car circuit, bringing the total number of races to seventeen and the total prizes to nearly fifteen million dollars.

Prize money is distributed through the two major race organizations, the United States Auto Club (USAC) and Championship Auto Racing Teams (CART). USAC was formed in 1955 when the American Automobile Association decided to quit sanctioning automobile races. With headquarters in Indianapolis, USAC sanctions the Indianapolis 500 and directs competition in championship (Indy cars), sprint and midget cars, as well as in stock-car

1986 Accessory Awards	
Bell Helmets	$ 9,000
Robert Bosch	68,000
Brake Systems	10,000
Canon	6,500
Champion	68,000
Duracell USA	5,000
Earl's Performance	6,750
GT&T Racing Products	5,000
Ideal Division	5,000
Koni America	5,000
Mallory Ignition	15,000
Mobil Oil Corp.	15,200
Monroe Auto Equipment	13,000
Pennzoil	165,000
PPG Industries	6,000
Premier Industrial	10,000
Rockwell International	10,000
Sears Diehard Battery	10,000
Simpson Sports	10,000
Snap-on Tools	5,000
Stant	5,000
Stewart Warner	5,000
STP Filters	5,000
STP Oil Treatment	17,000
Valvoline	15,000
Vandervell	8,000

Position	Points
1	
2	20
3	16
4	14
5	12
6	10
7	8
8	6
9	5
10	4
11	3
12	2
	1

Races	Purses
Indianapolis	$4,000,000
Michigan (two races)	1,150,000
Phoenix (two races)	800,000
Long Beach	700,000
Meadowlands	700,000
Montreal	700,000
Pocono	700,000
Portland	600,000
Toronto	600,000
Miami	550,000
Cleveland	500,000
Elkhart Lake, Wis.	500,000
Laguna Seca, Calif.	500,000
Lexington, Ohio	500,000
Milwaukee	450,000

racing. In 1979 car owners in the championship division withdrew from USAC, forming their own organization, CART.

CART is structured in much the same way as other major sports organizations such as the National Football League and the National Basketball Association. There are only twenty-four CART franchises. Initially franchises went for $20,000 each, but the price has since risen to $60,000. Car owners who hold a franchise get $7,000 "appearance money" from CART for each event they compete in. To maintain their franchise, owners must compete in eighty percent of the CART events. Making the entire seventeen-race schedule would bring a franchise holder $120,000 in appearance money. Teams without a CART franchise are welcome to compete at CART-sanctioned races, but they aren't eligible for the $7,000 guarantee. Non-franchise holders are, of course, also eligible to win prize money. Excluding special awards or accessory prizes, the guaranteed worth of events on the 1986 championship schedule, including the USAC-sponsored Indianapolis 500, ran from over four million to a half-million dollars.

In addition to these prizes, there is the national championship, determined by accumulation of points over the course of the season. At each race, points are awarded according to the order of the finish, ranging from twenty points for first place to one point for twelfth. Drivers who are among the top twenty in point standings at the end of the season share in the points bonus fund, which amounted to $1.2 million at the end of the 1986 season. When Al Unser Sr. won the 1985 National Championship in Miami, it earned him and Penske Racing an extra $300,000. Al Unser Jr.'s second-place finish earned him and Shierson Racing $200,000.

A Word for the Sponsors

While the prize purses and accessory awards keep growing, no car owner can run a serious championship team without the support of the various corporations that sponsor racing. Several of these companies, PPG Industries, Goodyear Tire and Rubber, and Valvoline deserve the special thanks of all racers and race fans.

PPG Industries (which was once known as Pittsburgh Plate Glass) makes paints, glass, fiberglass and chemicals, and is the official sponsor of the PPG Indy Car World Series. Its annual contribution to the series is more than two million dollars. To help dramatize the quality and performance of American-built automobiles, PPG works with the four major U.S. car manufacturers, fielding a team of specially prepared high-performance pace cars to pace all of the CART-sanctioned races.

At each event (including Indy), PPG awards $5,000 to each finisher, so even teams that don't finish high enough to participate in the prize purse at least get enough money to pay their hotel and food bills. PPG maintains a hospitality area for the race teams and the media at each CART event, and the areas always feature a first-class buffet. Crewmembers, who once subsisted on racetrack hot dogs, now have good food provided for them.

The man who handles the racing circuit for PPG is Jim Chapman. I first met Jim in the 1940s when he convinced Ford Motor Company to underwrite a tour featuring Babe Ruth for the benefit of American Legion Baseball. While Chapman and PPG have spent vast sums to support auto racing, he has yet to ask for a free ticket.

High-speed auto racing wouldn't be possible without the tires developed by Goodyear. The company supplies the teams competing at Indianapolis with free tires, but for the rest of the season, the teams pay about $850 per set—and even at that price, it's a substantial loss for Goodyear.

Like Goodyear, Valvoline provides essential services. Valvoline President Jack Boehn firmly believes that the company's association with racing has established high credibility for Valvoline products around the world. It takes oil to lubricate race engines and methanol to power them. Valvoline is practically the only supplier of methanol. The company operates a "filling station" in Gasoline Alley at Indianapolis, and at the other tracks it provides a tanker to fill the fuel tanks in the pits. About eighty percent of the teams receive fuel and oil free, while teams using and promoting a competitor's oil are supplied with the methanol at manufacturer's cost.

At Indianapolis, there are more than sixty other businesses and individuals who contribute to the race purse, giving cash prizes and "accessory awards." Their contributions add more than $750,000 to the stakes available at Indianapolis. For example, there's the lap prize fund. It's long been a practice to award a cash prize to the leader of each lap. Currently, the lap prize fund at Indianapolis totals $90,000, or $450 per lap.

Individual team sponsorships have long been a part of racing. Through most of the first sixty years of the Indianapolis 500, however, sponsors were almost exclusively companies with auto-related products. Champion Spark Plug Company, for instance, is the longest continuous sponsor at Indianapolis. But this has changed dramatically in the last decade as companies with a wide spectrum of products have found the Speedway, and auto racing, to be an effective marketing tool.

Anheuser-Busch, the St. Louis-based brewer of Busch, Budweiser and Michelob, is typical. In the mid-1970s, the company began sponsoring stock cars on the NASCAR circuit. In 1978 it included Indianapolis in its sponsorship plans. The company has been associated with some of the sport's top drivers, including Pancho Carter, Johnny Rutherford and Mario Andretti. The association with Andretti produced a national championship for Anheuser-Busch in 1984, but car owners Paul Newman and Carl Haas accepted a deal worth ten million dollars over five years to advertise Beatrice Products on the side of their car instead of Anheuser-Busch's Budweiser beer. Anheuser-Busch then moved its sponsorship to the Truesports team, owned by the late Jim Trueman, whose driver Bobby Rahal won the 1986 race.

The cost of a corporate sponsorship is high, but the companies also benefit. While they don't share in any prize monies won by the car, they do receive exposure to the race fans who buy their products. Every close-up of a race car takes in the names of products, prominently displayed on the sides and hood of the car, the helmet of the driver, and the uniforms of the driver and pit crew.

For some companies, such as tobacco manufacturers who are restricted by law from purchasing advertising on television or radio, sponsorship is the only way they can get their names broadcast to the public. Tom Sneva's 1985 and 1986 Indianapolis entries were both backed by Skoal, the smokeless tobacco product of U.S. Tobacco. In 1986 Phillip Morris signed a deal with Patrick Racing for its Marlboro-brand cigarettes. Philip Morris hoped that Patrick's "Marlboro Special," with driver Emerson Fittipaldi at the helm, would earn frequent television close-ups—and it did.

Domino's Pizza, which promises speedy home delivery of freshly made pizzas, has put its corporate muscle behind Al Unser Jr. Thomas S. Monaghan, founder and president of Domino's, also purchased the Detroit Tigers baseball club, in 1983. But while his Detroit Tigers aren't allowed to show their corporate colors, Domino's has gotten high visibility through its sponsorship of Unser and of the Pocono 500. According to *The Sponsors Report*, a newsletter that monitors corporate exposure on national television, Domino's netted almost $350,000 worth of air time when it broadcast the Domino Pizza 500 on cable television.

Domino's has also offered a prize that has yet to be claimed. If one driver wins all three 500-mile races in the same season—Indianapolis, Pocono and Michigan—the company has a cash award of one million dollars waiting.

The value a company derives from its sponsorship is more than how much media coverage it gets. Many sponsors design sales contests for their sales forces based on the "500" theme, with the winners receiving trips to Indianapolis for the race.

Important customers are invited to Indianapolis or to view other races on the circuit as guests of the company. Drivers make dozens of personal appearances at company-sponsored events. The race teams also maintain "show cars," usually a previous year's racing machine that can be displayed at trade shows and shopping malls.

While the vast majority of companies that come into racing as sponsors stay, shifting their allegiance when necessary as did Anheuser-Busch, the sponsorship equation is always open to reevaluation when a new management team comes to power inside a corporation. After owners Paul Newman and Carl Haas switched from Anheuser to Beatrice, Beatrice was purchased in a giant corporate takeover. The new president of Beatrice quietly bought out the contract with Newman, Haas and Mario Andretti. While the team is well-financed for a year or two, as a result of the changes at Beatrice the team is looking for a new sponsor.

Sometimes fate plays a hand in determining sponsorships. In the ill-starred 1964 race, Marathon Oil was the sponsor of driver Eddie Sachs, who was killed in the fiery crash that ended the use of gasoline at Indianapolis. As a result, Marathon, primarily a gasoline refiner, dropped out of racing.

Public Relations

It's ironic that a team's success at Indianapolis may be determined as much by its skill in the corporate boardroom as in the shop or on the track. Risk is not the long suit of most corporations. Yet risk—and the opportunity it brings—is an essential element of championship racing. The race driver of the future may be as much a corporate symbol as he is a daredevil. Already drivers who want to win races have had to add public relations to the considerable array of other skills needed to compete. Perhaps the handsome, gregarious Danny Sullivan, who knows his way around a camera as well as around the oval, will be the model for the next generation of drivers. It makes me wonder what will happen to the skilled, but shy, competitors like the late Bill Vukovich.

No driver gets to Indianapolis on enthusiasm alone. Big-time motor racing is an intensely professional affair—a business that functions like a sport, a sport that functions like a business.

Drivers and team owners alike know that at the level of the Indy 500, being a professional necessarily includes taking on many promotional duties not directly connected with breaking the lap record.

For a driver, it's necessary to promote oneself not only as a fast hand, but also as a temperate, responsible personality who can be trusted to handle himself positively in the public eye. As the years go by, motor racing's exposure in the news media continues to grow more intense, and with this increased exposure, the ability of a driver to represent his team and sponsor effectively has become essential.

To the major racing teams, sponsorship is indispensable. The teams depend almost entirely on corporate support to underwrite their season, for large as the Indy winner's purse is, totaling over half a million dollars in 1986, it's nowhere near enough to pay the annual expenses of building an Indy-car team—and even if it were large enough, there would only be one solvent team each year.

However, a race with the prestige and public exposure of the Indy 500 is an ideal forum for corporate publicity. Each year many of America's largest and most aggressive companies are happy to spend millions of dollars to ally their corporate image with the world's greatest motor race.

To attract the best of these corporate sponsors, car owners assemble the strongest possible combination of designers, engineers and technical personnel. They buy the most competitive racing hardware. And they search for the fastest and most "merchandisable" drivers they can find.

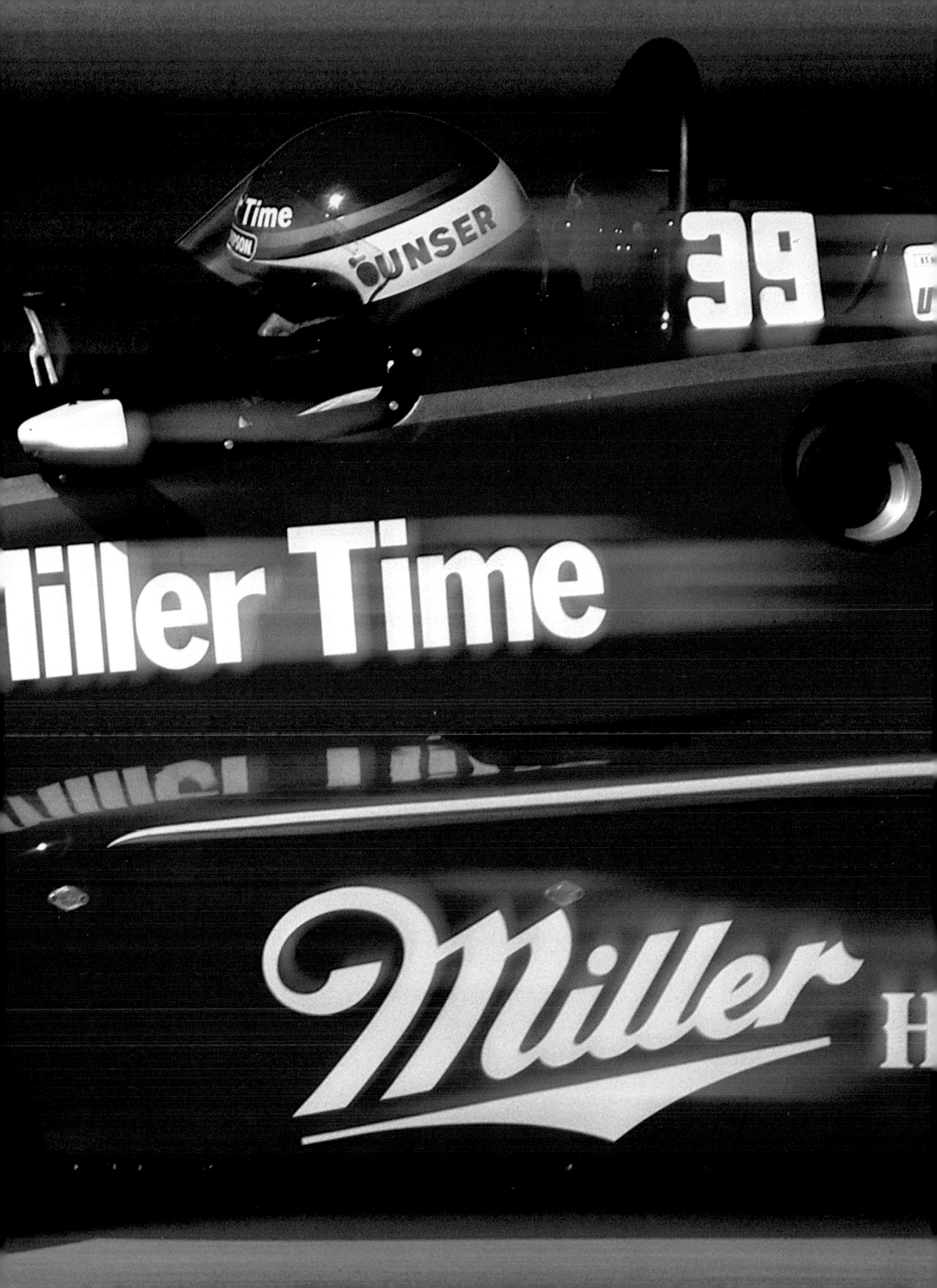
Time
UNSER
39
iller Time
Miller

Dick Simon Racing

COYOTE
A.J. FOYT ENTERPRISES

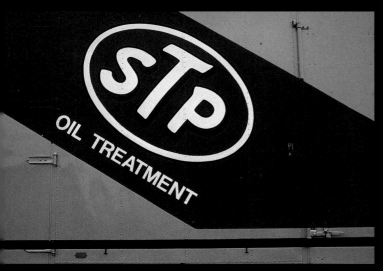

ARCIERO RACING TEAMS

DOMINO'S PIZZA

Delivers

DOMINO'S PIZZA TEAM

STP
OIL TREATMENT

7 ELEVEN

CALUMET FARM

CALUMET FARM

KRACO
CAR STEREO

BOSCH

PACE electronics

GURNEY CURB

CART

INDY CAR RACING TEAM

PPG

Race for Life

Miller

GOOD YEAR

SKOAL

BANDIT

CHEVROLET

GALLES RACING

Marlboro

GOODYEAR 1
PENNZOIL

Copenhagen
SNUFF

14 GILMORE
VALVOLINE

Goodwrench
PERFORMANCE PARTS
BUICK

Hertz
PENSKE

Pizza Hut

Living Well Fitness Centers
Lifecycle Aerobic Trainer

SCA WOLFF
TANNING EQUIPMENT
K CAR

Indy Car Team
GEOFF BRABHAM
ROBERTO MORENO
PANCHO CARTER

NEWMAN
RACING
RIO ANDRETTI
HANN

Budweiser

CANADIAN TIRE

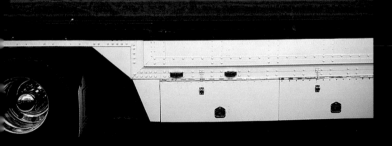

GOHR RACING
BUFFALO, NY INDIANAPOLIS, IN

OWNER-DICK HAMMOND
CHIEF MECHANIC-GALEN FOX

DURACELL
Dick Simon Racing

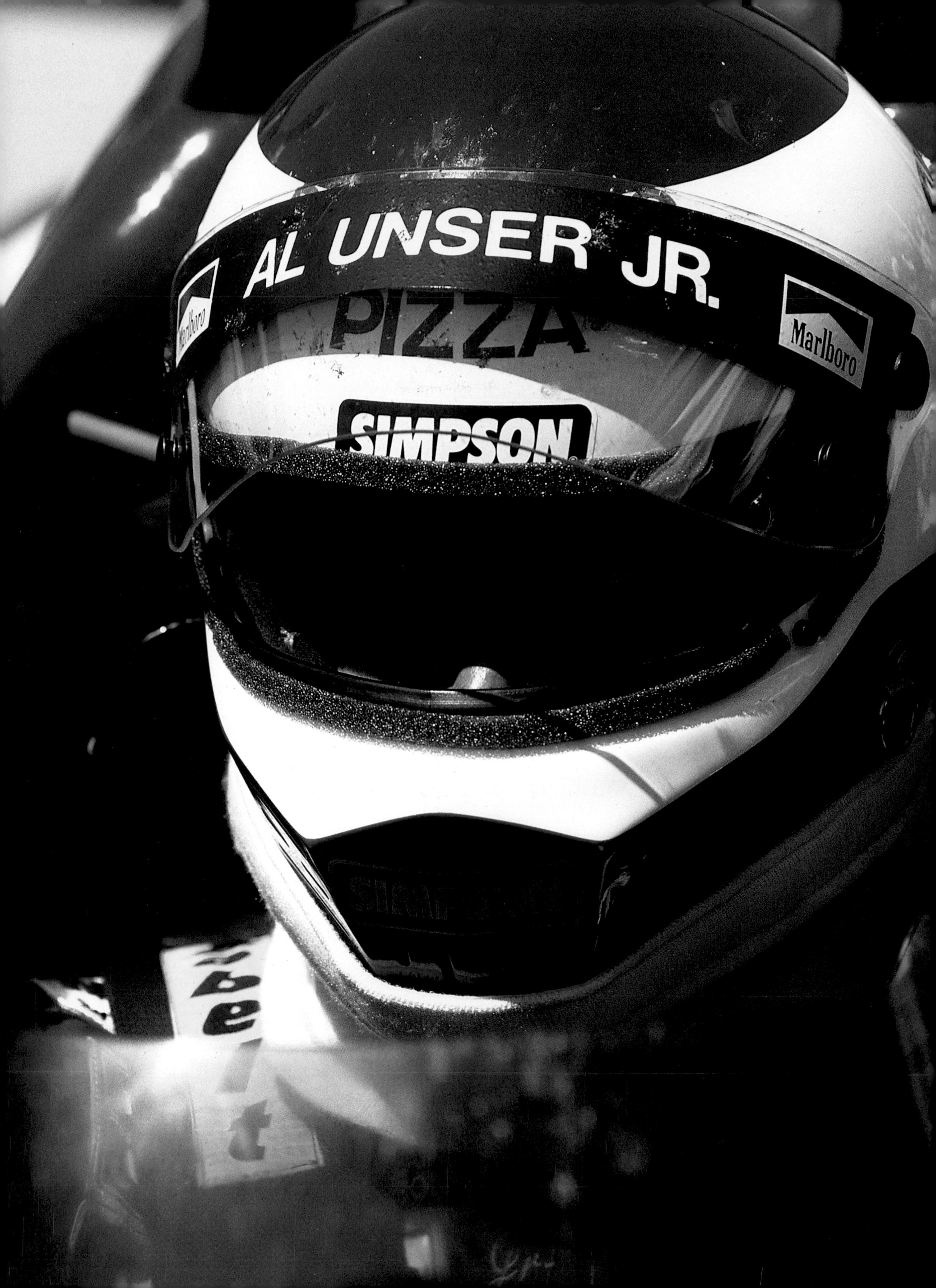
AL UNSER JR.
Marlboro
PIZZA
Marlboro
SIMPSON

Just as surely as modern Indy cars have become flying billboards designed to advertise their sponsors' presence, so too have the uniforms of the well-paid drivers who pilot them.

Every available square inch of a driver's helmet and driving suit has a logo or label of some kind affixed to it. The logic is that, while the photographer may only be taking a picture of the personality, the viewer is seeing the advertisement.

The matter of stickers and logos being properly placed on drivers and cars is so crucial that if a car gets an additional sponsor between qualifying and race day—as often happens—the professional photographers covering the 500 often must discard all earlier photos of the car. The presence or absence of one tiny sticker can identify a picture as being legitimately taken in the race, versus being taken some practice day earlier in the month.

For drivers and teams, of course, stickers and logos are a good deal more than a matter of mere authenticity —they're a crucial matter of dollars and contracts.

Like baseball, the Indy 500
thrives on the collecting of
statistics, trivia, historic
firsts.

One important historic first
occurred in 1977, when Janet
Guthrie (right) qualified for
the Indy 500. It was the first
time in the long history of
the race that a woman had
competed.

Inevitably, thanks to the
intense publicity
surrounding the 500, Guthrie
was a national celebrity
overnight. Though her result
in 1977 was a disappointing
twenty-seventh-place due to
mechanical problems, the
publicity she received that
first year, much aided by her
gracious manner and her
skill in dealing with
newfound notoriety, landed
her substantial sponsorship
in 1978. That year she
finished very well, in ninth
place, demonstrating to the
skeptics that a woman could
indeed withstand the severe
strain of this difficult race.

Her career at Indy included
one more race, in 1979, but
again she suffered early race
mechanical woes and
finished thirty-four. By
then, though, she'd made her
point, that women had their
place at Indianapolis just
just as surely, by then her
very businesslike sponsors
had made their point as well.

After successfully qualifying, and before the intensity of race day begins to loom, drivers and owners lounge along the pit wall, kidding, trying to relax.

There is still serious work to be done—the cars must be tuned for race day's crowded driving conditions, very different from the one-car-at-a-time conditions on qualifying day. But after qualifying, the pace of the work is relatively easy-going.

Between runs, Mario Andretti (left, above) chats with owners Paul Newman and Carl Haas, the latter chewing on his eternally unlit cigar—for smoking is forbidden in the pits at Indy.

Further up the pit lane, Roger Penske, Rick Mears and Al Unser Sr. kid with a member of the press (left, below).

In the working pits, owner Jim Gilmore (above) watches as A.J. Foyt fastens his helmet before going out for a fuel-mileage test. On race day, knowing exactly how many laps a car can run before needing to refuel may win or lose the 500.

But no matter what all the drivers and owners are doing, whether working hard or sitting along the pit wall joshing, the Indy elite are stars of the first magnitude.

Yet more than any other quality, it is their extraordinary celebrity that attracts sponsors.

With the arrival of a good sponsor comes a good budget—and the good budget buys the best hardware and pays the big salaries.

In the end, it's the all-important sponsor who puts a winner in Victory Lane.

Mario Andretti

Michael Andretti

Kevin Cogan

Emerson Fittipaldi

Tony Bettenhausen

Bobby Rahal

A.J. Foyt

Roberto Guerrero

Arie Luyendyk

Rick Mears

Jim Crawford

George Snider

Roberto Moreno

Danny Ongais

Johnny Rutherford

Al Unser Sr.

Speed

he quest for speed knows no limit, no boundaries. Build anything with wheels, and man will race it. To many, it's the ultimate challenge. It's always been so and if, in the process, the breed of racing machine is improved, so much the better.

Given a free rein, automobile engineers could build a car that would stick to the track at speeds of 250 or even 300 mph. But USAC stewards have been reluctant to risk the lives of the drivers by allowing the Indy 500 to become a competition of raw horsepower. Instead, they have restricted weights, engine size and chassis design in order to keep speeds from exceeding the driver's ability to drive safely.

A Fast Track

The ambitious Speedway founders began construction of a two-and-a-half-mile track in 1909 by laying down a surface of crushed stone held together by tar. When sprint races held that year proved that the track surface was unsatisfactory, the track was resurfaced with brick. Enough ten-pound bricks to fill some five hundred railroad cars were unloaded at the Speedway, and within ten weeks, the track had been completely repaved, giving rise to the Speedway's nickname, "The Brickyard."

In their era, the bricks made a fine surface. But increasing speeds soon showed that they weren't smooth enough and in 1937 the turns were paved with asphalt. Later, the backstretch was paved, and in 1962 the mainstretch received its asphalt covering. Owner Tony Hulman insisted that a yard of bricks remain at the start-finish line as a reminder of The Brickyard's heritage.

While the surface has been changed over the years, the measurements are still the same. The course is referred to as an oval but it is actually rectangular. The track is fifty feet wide on the straightaways and sixty feet wide in the turns. The corners are banked at nine degrees, twelve minutes. A steeper bank would allow higher speeds, like those achieved at the Daytona track (banked thirty-one degrees) and Talladega in Alabama (thirty-three degrees).

Speed Rules

Despite the relatively shallow banking, Indy cars could be made to go significantly faster than they do today, if not for USAC's restrictions. All Indy machines must have an open cockpit and a single seat, and the wheels must not be covered. The minimum weight for turbocharged cars is 1,550 pounds, and for non-turbocharged machines 1,475 pounds. This makes the Indy car much more robust than its Formula One counterpart, which weighs just over 1,200 pounds.

Air Force

Ironically, it isn't the lighter metal now used in frames, the more powerful rear-mounted engines or dollar boosts that have had the greatest effect on speeds. The secret ingredient is colorless, odorless and available free to everybody: air.

The two most significant changes in Indy-car design in the past decade and a half were the addition of wings in the early 1970s and the more recent utilization of ground effects. Jim Hall had a hand in promoting both of these innovations. While competing in the Can-Am Series races in the 1960s, the lanky Texan was the first to install front and rear wings—airfoils—on his car, a Chaparral. Grand Prix and Formula One teams picked up Hall's idea and European race cars soon sprouted wings of their own. What goes east across the Atlantic can come back west, and Team McLaren of England fielded the first Indianapolis entry with wings in 1970.

The wings of an aircraft create lift, which pulls the aircraft off the ground. The wings on a race car are installed "upside down"; that is, they create negative lift that pulls the car down onto the track. The cornering ability of a race car—how fast it can go through a turn without coming loose from the track and skidding—is a function of its weight and the amount of friction between the tire and the track. The downforce created by the wings adds many pounds of air pressure to the weight of the car, in effect making it two to three times heavier than it actually is. The wings, which weigh about twenty pounds, create thousands of pounds of downforce. The larger the wing area, the greater the downforce. A larger wing, however, does create drag, slowing the car down on the straightaways. But the increased downforce allows drivers to drive flat out through the turns. The net result is a higher average speed per lap.

Ground Effects

The late Colin Chapman originated the next major advance in aerodynamics—the incorporation of ground effects into racing machines. In 1978 after months of secret testing, Chapman unveiled the Lotus 78. Just as wings take advantage of the airstream moving over a car, Chapman's new chassis was built to take advantage of the airstream moving under the car. Chapman shaped the bottoms of the car's side panels into upside-down airfoils. Like the wings on the front and rear of the car, they generate downforce. The airfoils create areas of low pressure under the car, literally sucking the car to the track like a turbocharged vacuum cleaner. At high speed an Indy car generates more downforce than it weighs—it could actually adhere to an upside-down racetrack.

With Mario Andretti at the wheel, Chapman's ground-effects Lotus won the Formula One championship title in 1978. The very next year, Jim Hall entered another Chaparral at Indianapolis based on the ground-effects principle. Al Unser Sr. was the driver, and the Chaparral dominated the competition until a cracked transmission seal forced the machine out of the race at the halfway mark. Roger Penske's semiground-effects machine driven

by Rick Mears went on to win the 500. Entered again in 1980, however, Hall's Chaparral driven by Johnny Rutherford won the race.

Now, all Indianapolis entries are built using the ground-effects principle. As speeds have shot up, the concern of the race officials about the average speeds has also increased. The amount of downforce created by wings and underbody airfoils has been controlled by limiting the size of the wings and of the exit areas for air flowing under the car. This has at least kept speeds from leaping exponentially higher each year.

Tire Tracks

The blind fury unleashed by turbocharged engines has to be transmitted to the ground through the four little patches of rubber where the tires meet the track. Designing tires that will keep their grip on the track under the extreme forces generated by an Indy car is a highly developed science. The tires used on all cars at Indianapolis are donated to the teams by Goodyear, their manufacturer.

The tires, including the magnesium wheels on which they're mounted, weigh about twenty-eight pounds each; actually, they are ultra-thin tubeless rubber membranes with no tread (called "skin tires"). In competition, the tires last only about 110 miles. And they must be run on a dry track—even slight dampness can cause the cars to hydroplane. I've seen it happen at Indy: A sudden downpour will cause the tires to lose contact with the asphalt track and skim across the surface of the water.

On road courses in the U.S., the Indy cars run "rain" tires, as do Formula One cars. These special tires have a unique tread design that moves the water under the tire out of the way so the rubber can grip the pavement. Why not use them at Indy? The director of racing for Goodyear, Leo Mehl, explains, "In the rain, the wide tires create a huge spray. At Indianapolis, if five cars headed into a turn close together, the first two would come out. The three behind wouldn't be able to see through the spray to know when to turn."

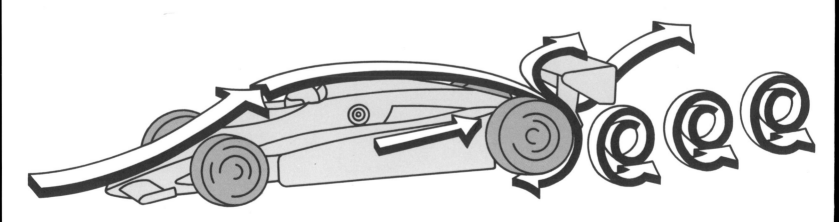

The diameter of the tires also affects the car's performance. Because the tires are made of bias (as opposed to radial) plies, they aren't exactly identical in size when taken from the mold. The teams experiment with tires of slightly differing diameters to find the combination of sizes that works best—a "magic" set. After that combination is found, a team may go through twenty-five to forty sets during practice to find a half-dozen sets with the same combination of sizes. The tires are mounted and a few practice laps taken to warm them up, then the diameters are measured. Those that measure the same as the magic set are stockpiled. The best-performing set of tires will be used to qualify the car, and that same set of tires must be used at the start of the race. That set, or one that closely matches it, will often be saved for the final pit stop to ensure perfect handling late in the race.

Bum Steer

When a car's front tires tend to slip as the car goes through a corner, the car is said to be understeering or "pushing." The driver has to turn the wheel further to compensate for the understeer. When the rear tires slip while the front tires are tracking properly, the car is oversteering, or is "loose." A car that's loose may appear to be tracking around a corner slightly sideways.

Oversteer and understeer can be adjusted by altering the distribution of the car's weight to the four wheels. This is done by adjusting springs and anti-rollbars in the suspension. When the car is neither understeering or oversteering, it is said to be "neutral." This fine-tuning of the suspension is the major task accomplished during practice.

Planned for Power

Like the chassis, the engines of Indy cars are carefully regulated. A Cosworth or similar engine is limited to 161 cubic inches of displacement—that is, the total interior volume of its cylinders must not exceed just over two-and-a-half quarts. A turbocharged motor, using a "stock" or non-racing engine block (such as the Buick engines introduced in 1984) can displace up to 209 cubic inches, while normally aspirated (without turbochargers) stockblocks displace 359 cubic inches.

Since 1968, most of the engines used at Indianapolis have been turbocharged. A turbocharger uses hot, rushing exhaust gases to spin a tiny turbine at speeds approaching 200,000 revolutions per minute. A shaft connects the turbine to a compressor wheel in an adjacent housing. The compressor compresses the fuel-and-air mixture before it gets to the cylinder; the compression means the cylinder can hold more fuel and air than it would if they were injected using atmospheric pressure alone. More fuel and air mean more power. To control the amount of additional pressure developed by the turbochargers, the rules require that Indy racing engines be fitted with a "pop-off" valve in the intake system, which diverts pressure when it exceeds nine pounds per square inch.

Although it has half the displacement of the V-8 engines commonly used to power American passenger cars in the 1960s and 1970s, a turbocharged Cosworth engine develops 750 horsepower, about three times the power of those V-8s. A Cosworth is good for about 600 miles of competitive driving; then it must be rebuilt, which costs approximately twelve thousand dollars. That's why most competitors start their run at Indianapolis with an engine just off the test stand.

Protective Cocoon

In the center of this mass of wheels, engine, plumbing, sidepods and drivetrain is the "tub," named for its resemblance to a common bathtub. Individually fitted to the driver, the tub is the driver's protective cocoon. He squeezes in and literally lies down in driving position. The fit is so tight that the steering wheel, tiny as it is, must be removed for the driver to get in or out of the car. Despite the tightness, a properly fitted racing machine is comfortable to drive. It's the speed in the turns that causes the discomfort.

Indy Aerodynamics
The powerful aerodynamics of the open-wheeled Indy 500 race cars virtually glues the cars to the track. The low nose and wings lift air over the car body and force air through side wings to hold the car to the ground.

Air coming from the top and sides of the car combines to push down on the rear wing. Air carries off the back of the car in a steady flow. The rear tires and wing create a swirling effect, or turbulence, which makes it difficult for racers following to control their cars.

A driver is subjected to the force of two and a half to three times the pull of gravity on every turn, four times per lap, eight hundred times if the car goes the whole race distance. Under that force, a driver's head "weighs" three times more than it does normally. Without the use of a helmet strap and a "horsecollar" neck brace, it would be impossible for a driver to hold his head upright against the side forces. The strap is attached to the left side of the helmet and then loops around the left arm, resting under the armpit. The horsecollar goes around the neck. The driver's head is literally tied on to his body; if it weren't, he'd be unable to keep his head upright in the turns.

Control Center

Once shoehorned into the cockpit, with the steering wheel installed after him and helmet strap, seat belts and shoulder harness fastened, the driver stares at the myriad of controls and gauges: ignition switch, tachometer, temperature gauge, oil temperature gauge, oil pressure gauge, turbocharger boost gauge, turbocharger boost control, front and rear sway bar controls (to regulate chassis roll), brake balance knob (to put more brakes on the front wheels or more on the rear), weight-jacking control (to adjust the spring rates on all four wheels, controlling stability), fire extinguisher release (to activate the on-board fire extinguisher) and radio talk-back switch (for communication with the pit).

Perhaps the final word on an Indy driver's working conditions was offered by Kevin Cogan during the closing minute of the 1986 race. ABC television had wired him for a radio hook-up during the competition. Cogan had a narrow lead over second-place Bobby Rahal going into Lap 193 when the yellow flag came out. The ABC announcers instantly made contact with Cogan to ask his strategy for staving off Rahal and Mears. Dealing with turbulence, the force of gravity and speeds of more than 200 mph in traffic, Kevin replied politely: "I'm a little busy right now. Talk to you later."

Race day morning—it arrives like a needle in the stomach. Nothing about the car feels right. . . . Or everything about the car feels right . . . flawless, perfect . . . as good as men can make it.

More likely, of course, neither is quite true. More likely, in the sweaty, hot nervyness before the start, the driver just needs something—anything—to believe in, to hold onto. At this moment, it's all he has . . . belief.

The nervyness builds and builds. There is commotion all around. The band is playing "On the Banks of the Wabash" as they push the car out of the pits to the starting grid. Its tires pop and crackle on the grit of the pit lane—an irritable sound.

The sun is already too warm. The air is too heavy with humidity. The driver's suit, made doubly uncomfortable by the full set of flame-proof long-johns underneath, is already soaked through with perspiration. The race will be dizzying, exhausting. It always is.

And chances are great that right now, hidden from view and impossible to detect, some tiny defect lurks deep within the car that will delay it in the race . . . perhaps prevent it from finishing—maybe even cause it to go hurtling out of control at 220 miles an hour, flying through the air to total destruction.

If only that one problem piece, hidden in the car as it sits on the grid right now, could be identified . . . if only it could be replaced this minute, before it's too late . . .

But there is no way to find it now. Only starting the engine, stressing the car to the maximum for as long as it will tolerate it—or until 500 miles have passed beneath its wheels—will answer this horrific, haunting question.

Forty-five minutes to go. The answer will come soon.

The High Priests of Speed,
like other high priests, live
by solemn ritual. Before
getting into the car,
everything must be done
correctly. Emerson
Fittipaldi (right) adjusts his
"Balaclava," the flame-proof
mask worn beneath the
helmet, carefully puts on his
flame-proof driving gloves,
pulls their gauntlets over the
sleeves of his driver's suit.

He steps over the bodywork
onto the seat cushion, one leg
at a time. Steadying himself
on the sides of the cockpit, he
slips his legs down into the
narrow nose cone.

In the extremely tight fit, he
can hardly move. His
crewmen must fasten his
belts for him. The belts are
pulled as tight as they will
go, for the less movement the
driver is subjected to in a
bad crash, the better chance
he has.

Finally, the steering wheel is
put in place and the foam-
cushion headrest is fitted
between the helmet and the
rear of the cockpit.

He is ready to race.

One by one, the other
combatants come up to the
starting grid. In 1983 Rick
Mears's Penske chassis
(top) gets a push from the
crew before the start. The
Newman/Haas Lola of
Mario Andretti (bottom)
rolls up to the grid in 1983.

All rise in silence as the Purdue University Band plays the National Anthem. Hundreds of thousands are motionless, hands folded.

The Invocation is read, asking God's blessings on this nation, this people, this race.

A moment later, in homage to American war veterans on this Memorial Day, a solo bugle sounds "Taps" . . . but could it be? Does this lonely bugle sound only for the past? Or in these fevered moments immediately before one of the most dangerous auto races on earth . . . does it sound for us!

No time to think of that now.

Ten minutes to go. This is what we came here for. We're here to race 500 miles. The first one to go that far is the best—those are the rules. Everything else is just talk. . . .

Somewhere in another world, a man sings "Back Home Again in Indiana." In that same far-off world, a crowd begins to roar . . . but it has nothing to do with reality now. Reality is a steering wheel and gauges ahead of you. A safety harness that pins your shoulders and torso tight to the car.

The outside world slips further behind. The last thing you hear is a woman's voice—Mary Hulman (bottom)—intoning the only words in the universe yet remaining to be said:

"Gentlemen, start your engines!"

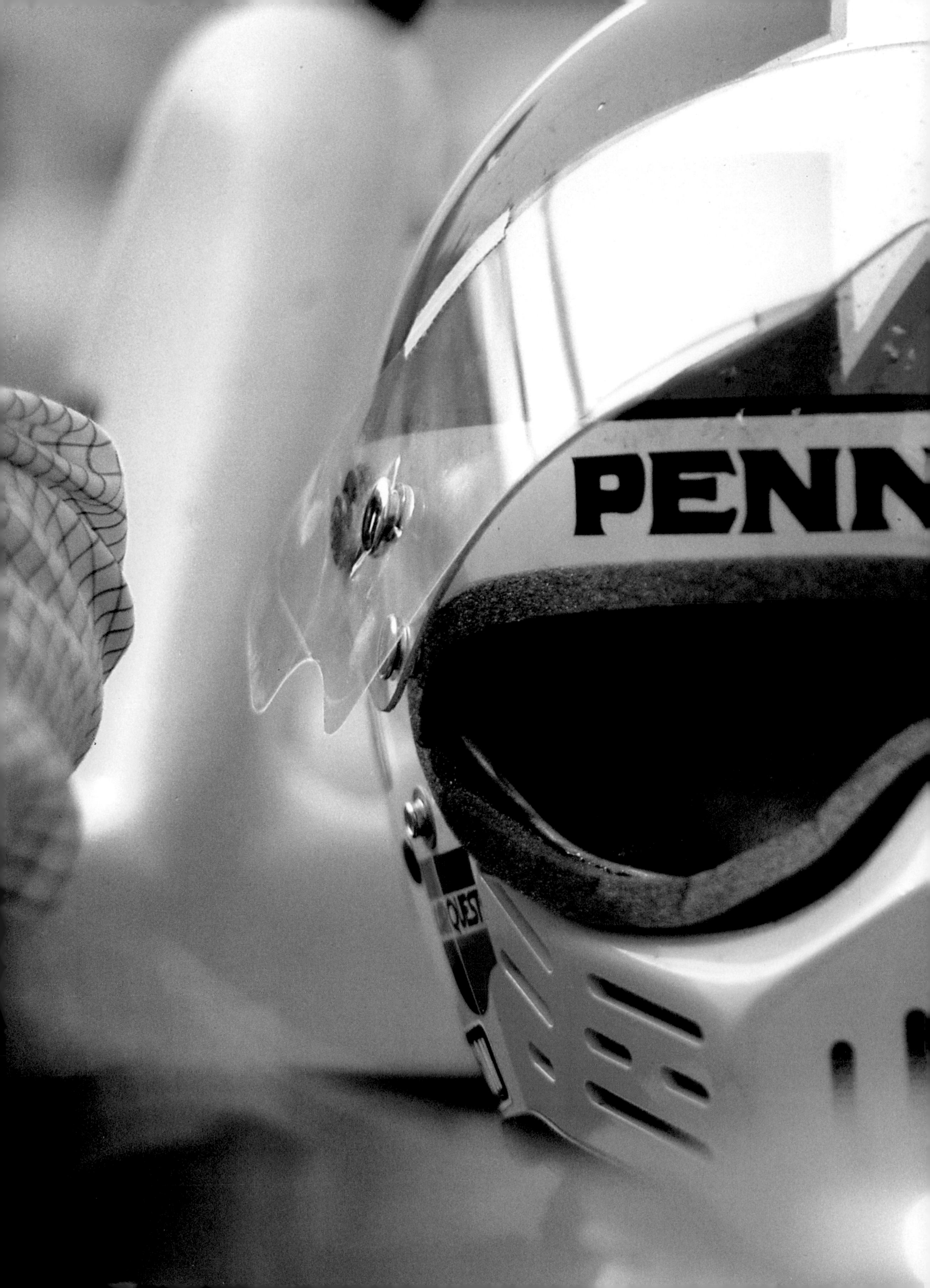
PENN
QUEST

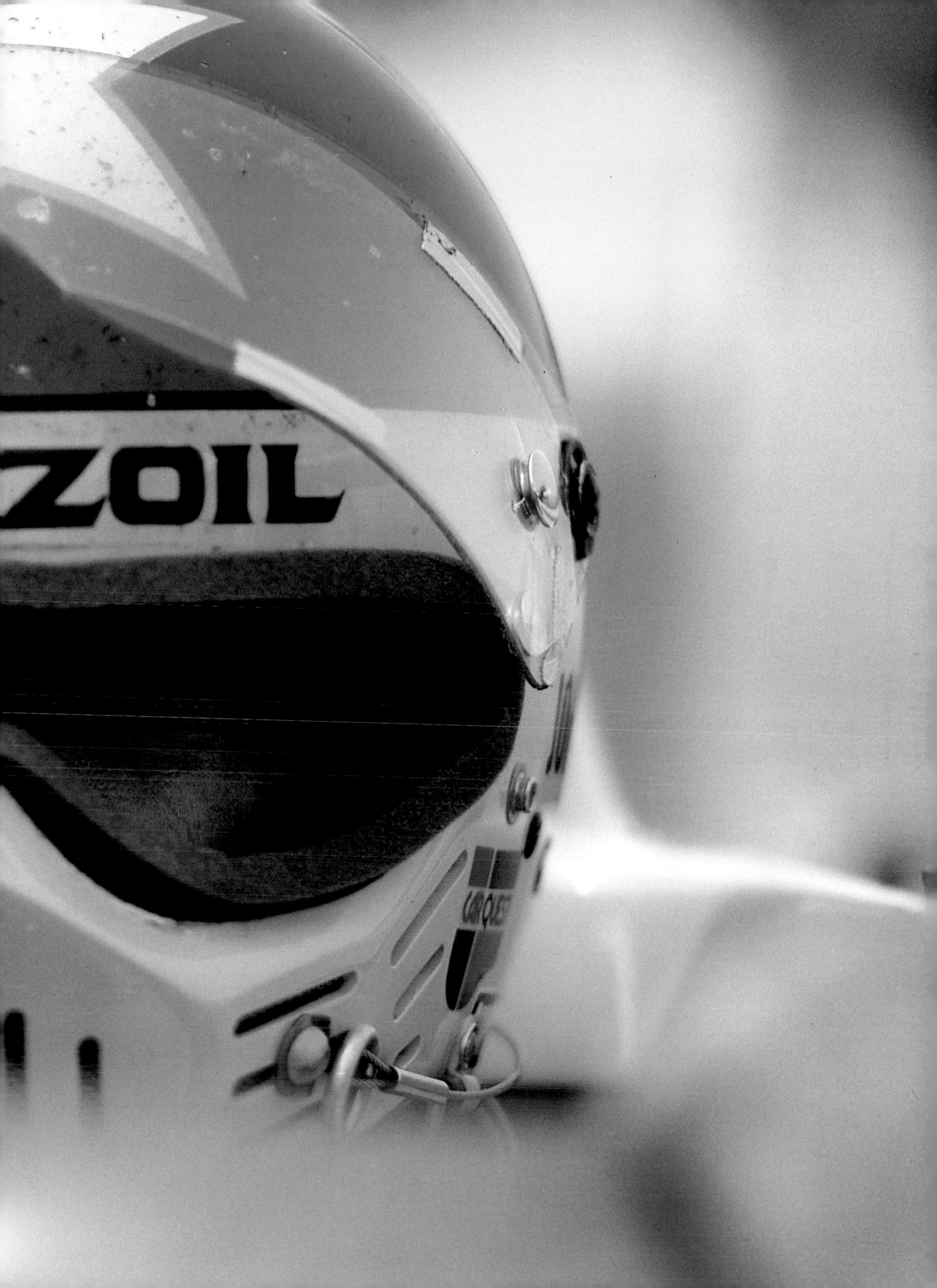
ZOIL

Gloves tight. Body snug.
Elbows tingling. . . . Run
the engine up rhythmically,
methodically.

Keep the oil circulating.
Engine temperature
climbing nicely.

Oil pressure good.

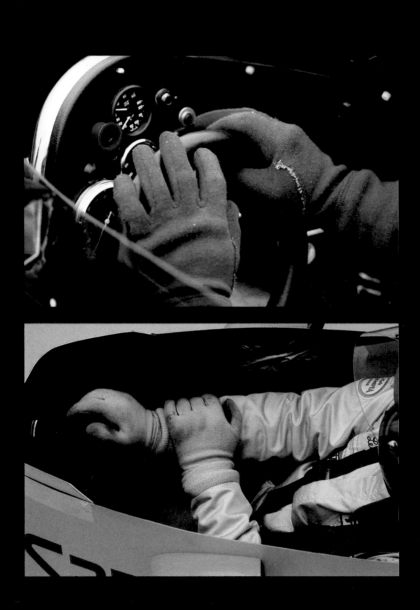

*...eartbeat racing—pulse
throbbing in your throat.*

*Mirrors okay. You can see
the car behind just fine . . .
but can't let him get ahead
. . . if he tries it at the start,
you'll . . .*

*No, the car ahead of you—
think about the car ahead.
Think of putting him in the
mirror.*

*Arms and legs tingling. Ice-
cold spikes streaking down
the back of the legs.*

*Getting ready, getting ready.
It's always like this—only
more so.*

*The Balaclava under your
helmet is soaking wet.*

*What did you forget?
Nothing, damn it. Let's go,
let's go!*

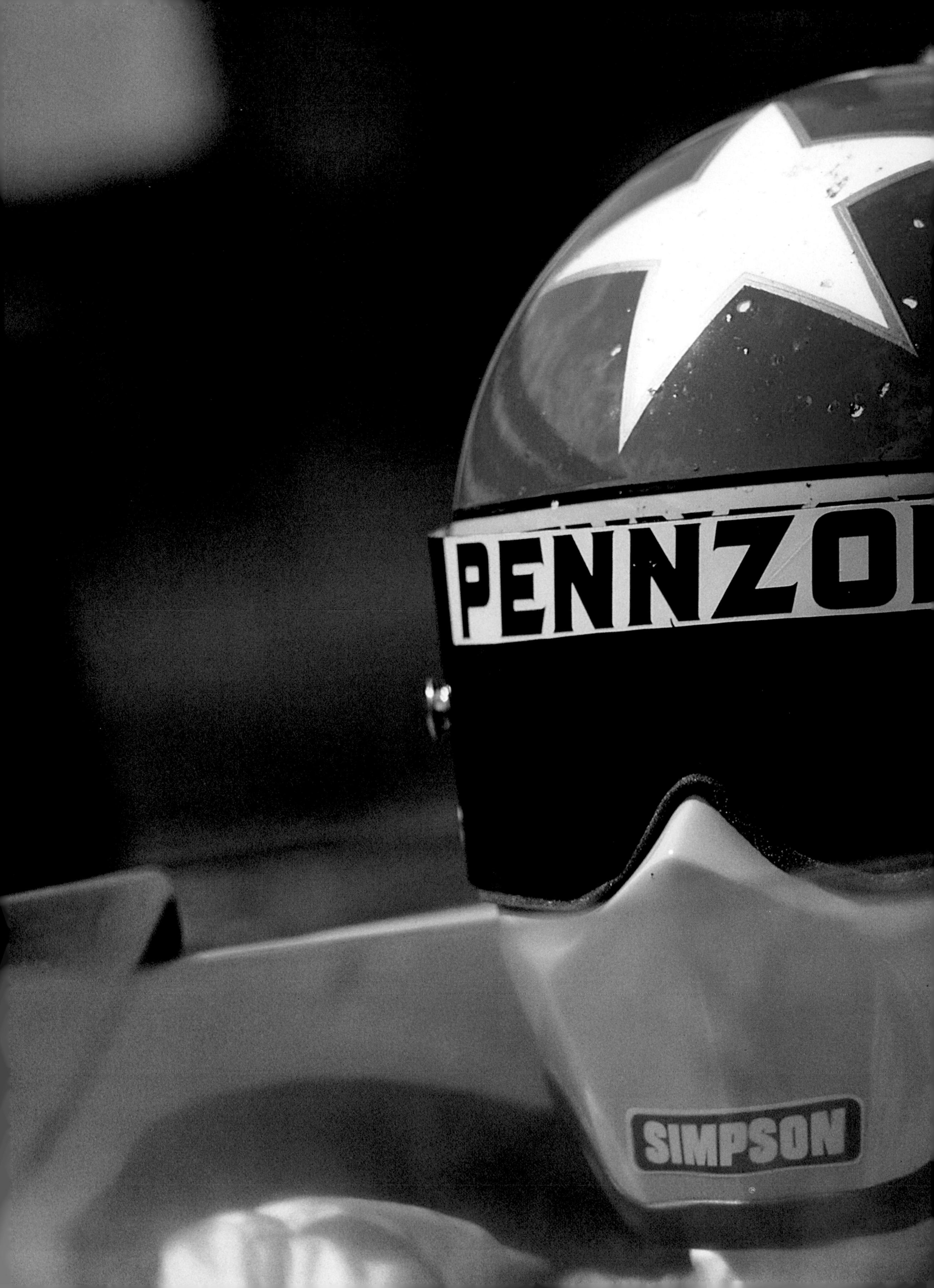
SIMPSON

The pace car and the other official cars filled with Speedway dignitaries move off the grid ahead. Gradually, with almost graceless slowness at first, the race cars follow, moving around the bend into Turn One.

Invariably, one car or another has trouble getting its engine started. And just as invariably, the crowd roars deliriously when its engine belatedly barks to life. It rushes ahead to claim its proper place in the formation.

At the end of the Parade Lap, the dignitaries' cars pull into the pit lane. Now, it is only the pace car and the racers.

The speed picks up, the racing engines now well warmed. The drivers zig-zag violently on the backstraight, bringing their tires up to operating temperature.

The infinitely large crowd along the front straight strains for the first view of them coming out of Turn Four . . . and here they are! The first three or four rows are well aligned. They're led forward by the pole-sitter.

Behind, cars struggle to line up coming out of the fourth turn—they don't want to lose too much ground as the sprint begins up the front straight.

196

*And in an instant, all other
sound vanishes. The massed,
raging shriek of 25,000
horsepower rushes down the
front straight (overleaf) in
one insane knot. Cars dart
madly to and fro, with
blinding speed, each
determined to pass at least
one other before the narrow
bottleneck of Turn One.*

1983 Teo Fabi/Scott Brayton▲ 1984 Al Unser Jr.▼　　1986 Bobby Rahal▲ 1983 Al Unser Sr./Rick Mears▼

500 miles. 2,000 turns. In spite of long slow-paced caution periods under the yellow light, in spite of the necessity of coming to a dead stop in the pits for fifteen-second fuel stops at least seven times . . . in spite of all this, the winner averages as high as 170 mph for the entire 500 miles.

Through grueling heat.

Enduring constant physical

In an Indy car, side-loading in the turns makes a 180-pound man weigh 540 pounds. Aerodynamic turbulence when following another car at 220 mph batters the driver like a professional boxer's best left jab—and worse still, can punch the car violently off-line in Indy's high-speed turns.

To go fast at Indy with the track all to yourself is a desperately dangerous enterprise—but to race other cars at Indy is infinitely more demanding. You must drive at the same desperately dangerous speeds, while also coping with a constantly changing track, the violent turbulence caused by other cars, the progressive changes in your own car as fuel weight decreases and tires begin to wear away.

1986 Randy Lanier▲ 1984 Tony Bettenhausen▼ 1983 Gordon Johncock▲ 1985 Danny Sullivan/Mario Andretti▼

Finally, you must know how to make the sudden maneuvers in turbulence that are necessary to overtake other cars, while still not losing control of your own car. A thoroughly chilly business.

Yet year in and year out, thirty-three drivers can be found who believe they know how to do all that. In 1983 pole-sitter Teo Fabi (top row, far left) proves his ability by getting past Scott Brayton.

During the 1985 race, in perhaps the most spectacular display in recent years of what can happen during a pass, Danny Sullivan (bottom row, far right) overtook Mario Andretti (shown following Sullivan here) in Turn One, immediately spun and very nearly crashed. He was able to continue, however, re-passed Andretti later and went on to victory.

In 1986 Bobby Rahal (top row, second from left) made the most dramatic pass in decades, getting by Kevin Cogan with only two laps remaining, to win the 500.

While the driver struggles every second of the way to gain an advantage on the track, his team busily monitors his progress. Pit boards let him know what his position is, how close his nearest competitors are, and whether he is gaining or losing ground.

Sometimes the pit board will inform him of his lap times so that he can adjust his speed according to the team's overall strategy—for after all, a 500-mile race is no short sprint. Conserving fuel and speed for the final stages has been the secret of many an Indy 500 victory.

Fuel mileage is carefully
calculated by each team.
When a car's tanks are
nearly empty, the team
makes sure the driver knows
it by giving him the "IN"
signal. The next time
around, he will come to the
pits and refuel.

Then he's back on the track
again (overleaf), doing what
he does best—going
absolutely as fast and as far
as skill, determination and
racing luck will allow.

The laws of physics play no favorites. Thanks to their color schemes, these four speeding cars all appear to be very different from each other—their teams and sponsors want it that way.

In truth, however, three are exactly the same model, while the fourth, though a different model entirely, is technically barely distinguishable from the rest.

The reason for this is simple enough. The demands of racing at Indy are the same for everyone, and therefore the laws of physics and aerodynamics, as currently applied, result in very similar solutions to the same problem.

*In 1984 Emerson Fittipaldi,
Pancho Carter and Danny
Sullivan (top left, bottom left
and bottom right) all drove
virtually identical March
84Cs.*

*Though at a glance hardly
distinguishable, the wild
card among the four is
Mario Andretti's car (top
right). Built in 1985 by
March's chief competitor, it
is a Lola T900.*

Champions

Indianapolis is not only the American auto race, it is an American event—a mixing pot and a great equalizer all in one. The international Grand Prix circuit has an upper-crust "silver spoon" image among U.S. race fans, while stock-car racing has been dominated by "good ol' boys." But Indianapolis is an egalitarian event that plays no favorites: All types of men—and a very determined woman named Janet Guthrie—have been successful at Indy. The drivers range from A.J. Foyt, the intense Texan who's a good bet to win the race every time he starts, to Jim Clark, the gentlemanly Scottish Grand Prix driver.

Until recently, most championship events in the U.S. were run on oval tracks in contrast to the international Grand Prix, a series of road races. Since its earliest days, Indianapolis has attracted foreign drivers, but until Australian Grand Prix driver Jack Brabham finished ninth at Indianapolis in 1961, the 500 was the province of the master American oval-track drivers such as Wilbur Shaw and Louis Meyer.

Brabham's showing paved the way for a non-American invasion. Designer Colin Chapman brought his rear-engine Lotus cars and Grand Prix champion Clark to Gasoline Alley in 1963. Brazilian Emerson Fittipaldi, another Grand Prix champion, began racing at the Speedway in 1984. And while foreign drivers began to make their mark in America, U.S. drivers moved into the international road-racing circuit, notably at Mount Fuji, in 1968, and in a race held during the 1972 World's Fair in Montreal.

The skills required to drive an oval are significantly different from those required on a road course, and few men have been successful at both. Aside from Clark, the only man to win both the World Grand Prix Championship and the Indianapolis 500 is Mario Andretti.

Emerson Fittipaldi

The next man to own both Grand Prix and Indianapolis titles, however, may be Emerson Fittipaldi, who says that even a two-time World Champion can be a bit awestruck by Indianapolis. "I was very surprised. A lot of people, such as Jackie Stewart, had told me Indianapolis was a big event, but I had no idea how big until race day," the cool Fittipaldi explained. His first start at the Speedway came in 1984. "When I arrived at the track on race morning, I had never seen so many people in one place in my life."

But the differences between Grand Prix and Indianapolis go deeper than the size of the crowd. "To begin with, there is the painstaking setting up of the car. Then you must drive much more smoothly at Indianapolis because of the turbulence. When you're following a group of three or four cars at more than 200 mph, the turbulence is much worse than I had ever experienced on a road course. Learning these things takes time. You cannot rush at Indianapolis. Sometimes I have to control myself and say, 'Emerson, take it easy. It's a long race, there's still a long way to go.' "

Caution is the byword of Fittipaldi's driving style. The Brazilian can lead any race he's in, but he's not one to take chances. He is more concerned with crossing the finish line in one piece, than in being the fastest. During his second start at Indy in 1985 for Patrick Racing, even though he led for nineteen laps, he treated it as a learning experience. His goal was to keep the leaders in sight, not necessarily to win.

Fittipaldi says the length of the race, 500 miles compared to 250 or less for Grand Prix events, creates some difficulties for him, as do the dangers of the oval track. "In Grand Prix racing, there are no pit stops. The race starts, and you keep driving until it's over. This matter of pit stops, their timing and importance, is something I have to learn," he continued in his charming Latin-accented English. "Also, you can't make a mistake at Indianapolis and recover. In a Formula One car on a Grand Prix track, there's room to make a mistake. You can put the car sideways and still recover. At Indianapolis, if you go sideways, that's it. You are going to hit the wall or, if you're lucky, spin in the grass. Indy is one place you don't want to make mistakes. As I said, I have a lot to learn."

Fittipaldi, who won a world driving title for Colin Chapman and Lotus in 1972 and another for McLaren in 1974, is obviously learning how to drive on oval courses. After leading at Indy in 1985, he captured his first 500-mile victory at Michigan. In the 1986 Indy race, nursing a sick engine, Fittipaldi came in seventh, six places ahead of his previous year's finish.

Despite being relatively new to oval racing, Fittipaldi looks every inch the experienced, veteran racer. A weathered face features eyes that betray his intelligence and superb education. Indy-car racing is really a second career for Fittipaldi. After his success on the Grand Prix circuit, he returned to Brazil to form a national racing team. But South America proved just too far away from Europe to serve as a base for a successful effort.

During the racing season, Emerson lives in Key Biscayne, Florida. It's almost impossible to get to know a driver well during the hectic days leading up to the Indy 500, so I visited Emerson in 1985 at his home in Florida. I learned that his father, Wilson, is a sports broadcaster. Through his work at Grand Prix events throughout the world, he introduced Emerson to road racing. My goal now is to introduce Wilson Fittipaldi, who's still active in Brazil, on the microphones at Indianapolis.

Our talk naturally turned to the possibility that Emerson could become the third man to win both the Grand Prix driving title and Indianapolis. Mario Andretti, who won at Indy in 1969 and captured the world title in 1978, is a familiar rival of Fittipaldi's. They've driven wheel-to-wheel in a number of Formula One races over the years, and I asked Emerson about Andretti.

"Mario is not only one of the greatest race drivers I've ever competed against, but he's also a great sportsman," Fittipaldi replied quickly. "Mario could retire at any time. He has enough money to have a good life. He has two sons who are racing. But he keeps driving because he loves it. I really admire him. He's a good example for all drivers."

Mario Andretti

Though he may now be an inspiration to others, as a youngster there was little to encourage Andretti to become a racer. Mario was born in Trieste, Italy, in 1940. As a teenager, Andretti went to the movies to see the short newsreels about Formula One racing. These films sparked a dream. "I liked to dream," he recalls, "and I wanted to be like the men in the newsreels, to drive in a Grand Prix event."

In 1955 the Andretti family emigrated to the United States, settling in Nazareth, Pennsylvania. Within a few days of his arrival, Mario saw someone pull in to a filling station with a race car on a trailer. It was a sprint car—a primitive upright roadster fitted with an enormous engine. In broken English, Mario began questioning the car's owner. The men were headed for the local half-mile track for some practice. Mario and his twin brother, Aldo, followed. Before long they were attending sprint and stock-car races on a regular basis. It was a short step from the grandstand to the grease pit, and soon the two were racing. Within three years of his arrival in the United States, Mario was driving stock cars, and in the succeeding three years, he won twenty races.

A Winning Formula

Stock cars weren't Formula cars, and Mario moved on, arriving at Indianapolis as a rookie in 1965. Driving the Dean Van Lines Special, he set new lap records during qualifications, started in fourth position and crossed the finish line third. His style in those days was to put the throttle to the front bulkhead and just hang on.

Like many of his contemporaries, Mario knew the only way to make a name for himself was to go all out and take a few chances. His amazing start at

March 85C

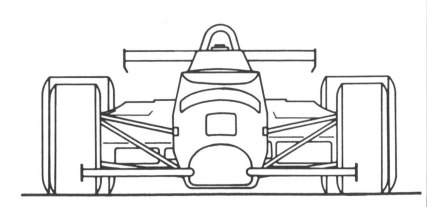

Indy won him enough votes to be named Rookie of the Year. While his driving style has become more cautious over the past two decades, he's still very, very fast.

The 1965 race was won by Jim Clark, driving for Lotus and Colin Chapman. Mario remembers talking at length with Clark at the track. "To meet him in the mid-1960s was very exciting. I had this hidden love for Grand Prix racing, so I was very interested in Clark and, through him, I met Colin Chapman as well. When I met Chapman, I talked with him about the Grand Prix and I said I'd like to try it. Chapman told me that when I was ready to drive Grand Prix, he'd have a car for me."

That conversation led to a Grand Prix championship for Andretti and Chapman in 1978. The association with Lotus brought Andretti his greatest Formula One success. None of these was more personally satisfying than his victory in the 1976 Italian Grand Prix.

Despite the World Championship and a string of victories on the Grand Prix circuit, Mario points out that much of his success can be traced to his first win at Indianapolis in 1969. He finished almost two laps ahead of the runner-up, Dan Gurney, setting a new record for average speed of more than 156 mph. "It's so important to win the 500," he later confided. "And if you can win it early in your career, it really sends you. It makes everything so much easier. Opportunities start knocking and doors open that never opened before."

Andretti took advantage of many of those opportunities, and for more than a dozen years flew all over the world to compete in major events, while also keeping an active schedule in the U.S. He has competed at Indianapolis every year since 1965, save one. That year, 1979, he drove in the Grand Prix of Monaco instead, seeking a second world championship.

This hectic travel schedule explains why Andretti has yet to win at Indianapolis for a second time. When rain washed out the first weekend of qualifying in 1978, Mario decided to race the next weekend in Belgium. A back-up driver qualified the car for Mario at Indianapolis but, according to the rules, Andretti was forced to start last in the field. He moved from thirty-third to finish ninth, and turned in the fastest lap of the race.

In 1981 Andretti faced another schedule conflict and had Wally Dallenbach qualify his car at Indianapolis. Again, he started in the last row on race day, yet he led for twelve laps and crossed the finish line second behind Bobby Unser. The race stewards awarded Andretti the victory the very next day. They penalized Unser a lap after ruling that he had passed several cars while coming out of the pits during a yellow flag. Unser appealed the decision and eventually was named the winner.

Now Mario has abandoned the Grand Prix circuit to devote himself to Indianapolis and the championship races in the United States. He has another reason to confine his racing to America. He can better guide the driving careers of his sons, Michael and Jeff.

In 1984, the same year he won the national championship, Mario and son Michael started Indianapolis in the same row. Michael actually outqualified his dad, averaging a half-mile per hour faster over the ten-mile qualifying run. Michael started fourth, on the inside of the second row, while Mario started in sixth position on the outside of the same row. In that race, Michael shared Rookie of the Year honors with Roberto Guerrero— the same title his dad had won in his first Indy twenty years earlier.

In 1986 Michael not only outqualified his dad— starting in the front row, third position—but he came in fourth, after leading the race for forty-seven laps. Mario, who wrecked his car after qualifying, had to drive a back-up machine starting in the last row. The machine didn't handle right and Mario had to drop out after nineteen laps, leaving his son to carry the Andretti racing banner.

Jack Brabham

The intermixing of European Grand Prix and American oval-track racing was begun, ironically, by an Australian. When Jack Brabham arrived at the Speedway in 1961, he brought along a European-style road racing machine powered by a four-cylinder Cooper-Climax engine. Not only did it have just two-thirds the displacement of the Offenhauser engines used in the huge Indy roadsters, but the new engine was located *behind* the driver. The machine was promptly dubbed "the funny car" by Speedway regulars.

Brabham's machine weighed just over 1,000 pounds, compared to 1,600 pounds for the average roadster. While the car had less horsepower than the traditional roadsters, it was far lighter. Brabham qualified thirteenth and finished ninth. The surprising finish was the beginning of the end for the ungainly front-engine roadster.

Despite his revolutionary impact on the sport, Brabham was not personally flamboyant. Dark-complexioned and six feet tall, he seemed somewhat shy, especially considering that he'd already won a world championship before arriving at Indianapolis. Brabham retired in 1971 with three world championships to his credit. And he left another legacy to racing—his son Geoff began competing at Indianapolis in 1981. Jack Brabham usually shows up at the Speedway every year, unnoticed by present-day Gasoline Alley regulars. These days, they work on nothing but rear-engine cars, and they don't call them "funny."

Colin Chapman

The rear-engine race cars introduced to Indianapolis by Brabham were made popular by Briton Colin Chapman. Chapman's Lotus cars had been successful in Formula One racing in Europe, and he felt that a machine of that type with sufficient horsepower could challenge Indianapolis. In 1963 Chapman arrived at the Speedway with Team Lotus and drivers Jim Clark and Dan Gurney. He brought along two new low-slung Lotus cars designed especially for Indianapolis. They were powered by aluminum Ford V-8 racing engines.

Chapman referred to the conventional American racing engine, the Offenhauser, as a "four-cylinder vibrator." Chapman's machines borrowed from the tradition of light aircraft construction—each had a twin-tube ladder frame with the body's metal skin stressed for added support. Speedway regulars derided the cars, saying they were too light and too fragile for the rigors of the 500-mile course.

The Debutantes

Everyone's interest focused on the new Lotus creations and their drivers, Clark and Gurney. Clark qualified in the second row, while Parnelli Jones captured the pole, setting a new track record at 143.137 mph, only .5 mph faster than Jim Clark in the Lotus.

Parnelli and Clark dueled for the lead throughout the race. With just a dozen laps left, Parnelli's machine began to smoke. Chief Steward Harlan Fengler considered giving Jones the black flag for spraying oil—in effect ordering him off the race track immediately. But the car's owner, J.C. Agajanian, appeared at the starting line and engaged Fengler in a heated discussion. The black flag never appeared. After the race, Agajanian asserted that the smoke had been caused by oil from the car's oil reservoir dripping on the hot exhaust pipe.

Roger McCluskey, running in third place, spun out three laps from the finish. Roger, now a USAC official, blames his crash on the oil from Parnelli's car. McCluskey charges that "they had the black flag in their hands and Agajanian talked them out of it." Clark finished second. Colin Chapman and the Lotus crew took the black-flag incident as just one of the breaks.

Jim Clark

Clark returned the next year and was leading near the 100-mile mark when his tire threw a tread. The tread wrapped around the suspension, breaking it and ending Clark's race.

Based on his finish in 1963 and the showing in 1964, Clark was favored to win the 1965 event. He won

Lola T-86/00

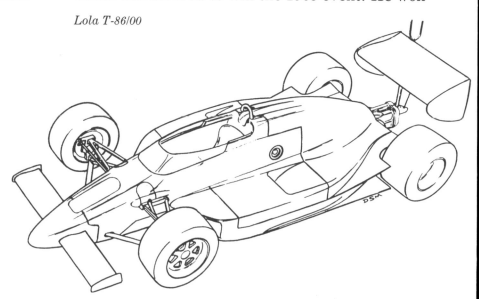

with ease, becoming the first driver to finish with an average speed over 150 mph. This time, it was Parnelli Jones who came in second.

Every movement on the track showed that Clark was in complete control of his car. His mastery over the car extended to the course—he drove as though guided by some sixth sense. Clark was not a daredevil. He led a lot of races and he finished a lot of races; the other drivers knew that if they made a move on Clark, he wouldn't do anything foolish to stop them.

The 1966 race spawned another controversy involving Clark. During the race, the Scotsman spun twice in oil. Each time he had the presence of mind to push in the clutch, keep the engine revving and let the car slide. Then, at the right instant, he popped it back in gear and kept moving. I'd never seen a driver pull out of spins like that before at Indianapolis. Cars that spin usually wind up against the wall or out of action in the infield.

From the press box I could see that Clark's coolness had kept him in front of the field. Toward the end, the driver's board on the straightaway showed that Clark was in the lead. I announced this to the crowd, who settled back to await Clark's second trip to Victory Lane. Clark's pit crew already envisioned him coming in first and Graham Hill, another world champion, in second. Then, just before the final lap, the driver's scoreboard changed. Although no one had passed Clark on the course, Hill was now listed in first place. I was stunned. I announced the correction to the crowd, fully expecting the scoreboard to change once more and show what I and the Lotus crew thought was a momentary mistake. But it never changed. The race ended with the board showing Hill ahead of Clark. Neither Colin Chapman nor sponsor Andy Granatelli filed an official protest, but years later, both were still convinced that Clark won the 1966 race.

The Flying Scotsman
It was after the victory in 1965 that I took off for Scotland to work on a motion picture about this quiet champion. The title, *The Flying Scot*, recalled the name of the famous British express train. The film detailing Clark's story was shown later that summer on American network television.

Visiting Clark in Duns, Scotland, my first stop was the home of his parents, a huge estate located on the border between England and Scotland. His mother confided, "We used to worry all the time when Jim was racing. But he's getting to be a better driver now and we don't worry so much."

Jim met us at his own farm, located nearby. Clark had deep, piercing black eyes that could seemingly see through you in an instant. Moving out into the fields, Jim told us, "If racing never paid me a dime, I'd be racing today." Then he added, "But my father, being Scottish, felt that as long as I was racing, I might as well get paid for it."

I continue to remember Jim's housekeeper remarking, "I always listen to Jim's races on the wireless, but I do wish he'd get married and come home and fix up the kitchen." That wish was never fulfilled. In April 1968, Jim was killed in a minor race at Hockenheim, Germany.

A.J. Foyt
The success of men such as Jim Clark, Jackie Stewart and Graham Hill made Texan A.J. Foyt vocal in his chagrin that so many American race purses were going to Europeans. And he took it upon himself to change racing history.

When Foyt walks into a room, all eyes turn toward him. He's a big man, just shy of six feet tall but with a stocky body that has gone over 200 pounds at times. He has an intense desire to be the best and to be known as the best. To Foyt, coming in second place is losing—and you never have any doubt about his feelings.

The outspoken Foyt reminds me of one of his friends, Bobby Knight, who coached the University of Indiana to win several NCAA basketball titles and the U.S. Olympic basketball team for a gold medal in the 1984 games. The two have a lot in common. Both men are willing to work twenty-four hours a day for victory, do not hesitate to let you know their feelings, and exhibit an intense loyalty to the people and principles they believe in. I admire these traits, but they've created both very loyal followers and very vocal critics.

Knight tells how he and Foyt encountered a disgruntled fan after the Hoosier Hundred auto race at the Indiana State Fairgrounds. Foyt had finished second, and he and Knight were commiserating. A spectator leaving the grandstand saw the two and shouted, "Well I'll be damned, there they are together, the two most obnoxious men in sports." Knight and Foyt replied in unison with a single unequivocal word.

Foyt was driving me through the streets of downtown Houston several years ago, pointing out along the way property and buildings he owned. "When I picked my business manager, I told him that if I ever went bust and was out on the road hitchhiking and he passed me driving a Rolls Royce, I'd catch up with him and drag his rear from one end of Texas to the other."

Whatever he said to his business manager must have worked, because Foyt has been as successful off the track as on it. He maintains a home in a stylish section of Houston as well as a 1,500-acre ranch northwest of the city. The ranch reminds me of a plush Kentucky thoroughbred farm, and in fact Foyt keeps over a hundred thoroughbred race horses in his stables. Foyt bought the ranch in the mid-1970s after a serious pileup in a stock car at Riverside, California, threatened his racing career. A.J. has added an enormous mansion, its rooms sprinkled with auto-racing trophies.

It always bothered me that Foyt could win a half-million-dollar purse at Indianapolis one week and then compete at some obscure dirt track the next. "You have to remember that when I started racing I had no money," he explained. "I slept in my car and had trouble getting together enough money for food. Some of the promoters helped me out with cash, and I've never forgotten them. This is my way of paying them back."

Racing Luck

Foyt won his first Indy in 1961, and since then has added four more wins and has led the race no less than thirteen times. The 1961 victory was something of a surprise, even for the self-assured Foyt. The Texan was leading Eddie Sachs by a full ten seconds when his crew called him into the pits. His fueling apparatus had malfunctioned on his previous pit stop, and he needed more fuel if he was to finish the race. Sachs went speeding by when Foyt stopped, moving to the front with a lead that virtually guaranteed a win.

With just five laps to go, Sachs felt his car lurch. Looking back, he saw rubber peeling off his right rear tire. It was obvious that Sachs was in trouble, and the commotion in his pits confirmed it. Sachs had just a few seconds to make a critical decision. If he went on, the tire might hold and victory would be his. If he stopped for a new tire, he would finish no better than second. With just three laps left, Sachs entered the pits. A new wheel went on quickly, but Sachs lost to Foyt by eight seconds. After the race, Sachs explained his heart-breaking decision by saying, "It's better to be second than to be dead." Foyt chalked up his first Indianapolis victory to racing luck.

Team Effort

Not content to stay behind the wheel, Foyt began building his own race cars, called Coyotes, and running his own race teams in the late 1960s. Like Mario Andretti, he included the Daytona 500 stock-car classic in his list of victories, adding credence to the belief that Foyt can win in any car on any kind of track.

Foyt, now past the age of fifty, is still a favorite at Indianapolis every time he enters. And Indianapolis is quite a favorite with Foyt. He and the late owner, Tony Hulman, were close friends. Rumors were always afloat that Foyt wanted to own the Speedway. While presiding at the Victory Dinner after Foyt's fourth win in 1977, I heard A.J. say to Tony as he was handed his pay envelope, "Why don't I just leave this with you as a down-payment on the Speedway?" Hulman just smiled.

In addition to determination and skill, Foyt has another asset that is envied by his rivals on the race track. For a dozen years, Foyt has worked with sponsor Jim Gilmore, whose name appears next to A.J.'s on the Gilmore Foyt Racing entries. Driver Gordon Johncock got Gilmore involved in racing. Johncock was building a race car in Hastings, Michigan, about twenty-five miles from Gilmore's home in Kalamazoo. Johncock signed Gilmore Enterprises as a sponsor, and the alliance continued with Johncock for several seasons, until 1972. When rumors of the split spread, twenty-six teams contacted Gilmore, but Jim heard that Foyt might be interested in a sponsorship arrangement. A contract—renewed each year—soon launched a very profitable partnership.

Gilmore and Foyt are much more than simply sponsor and team owner: Gilmore participates financially in the entire racing enterprise. And, Jim adds, "I guess A.J. is my best friend." Gilmore's reasons for staying with the venture go far beyond business. "Racing is my whole life," he says. The car in which Foyt won the 1977 race sits in a recreation room at Jim's house in Kalamazoo.

Louis Meyer

While Foyt was prominent at the anniversary celebration held on the first day of qualifications in 1986, he shared the spotlight with the Speedway's first three-time winner, Louis Meyer. Quiet and unassuming, Meyer won his third and final victory in 1936. When he was elected president of the 500 Old timers Club several years ago, Meyer turned down the honor, taking a role as vice-president instead.

Meyer was just twenty-three when he won the Indy 500 on his first try in 1928. Starting in thirteenth position, Meyer captured the checkered flag in a race that lasted more than five hours. Today, the drivers take a little more than half that time to cover the same 500 miles.

March 85C

Meyer was absolutely fearless; he had to be, competing in an era when other drivers were dying all around him. Seeing all the crashes, knowing the men who didn't make it to the next checkered flag, his own enthusiasm for the sport never waned. The slim purses of the Depression years didn't scare him off either. It's a wonder that the 500 made it through the 1930s. Prize money was drastically reduced, and Meyer received just $18,000 out of a total purse of $54,000 for his second win in 1933. He beat Ted Horn to the finish line in 1936 and became the first driver to be given the pace car, a Packard, as part of his prize.

The third win must have been the charm for Meyer. He tried the Speedway again, but late in the 1939 race, he crashed. Meyer returned to the pits and resolved to quit driving then and there.

While he was never again behind the wheel on race day, Meyer's influence was felt by many Indianapolis winners over the next two and a half decades. Meyer and Dale Drake acquired the Offenhauser, the premier racing engine of the day, and set up a production facility in California. The engine had been designed in 1921 by Harry Miller, Leo Goosen and Fred Offenhauser. The name was changed to the Meyer-Drake "Offy" and the engine, and a modern variant of it, were used well into the 1970s until the Cosworth engine, designed and built in Great Britain, became the standard power plant for serious racers.

Meyer still follows the circuit, spending nearly six months out of the year in a motor home, traveling from track to track. He no longer has an interest in the engine company, but he still loves to go racing, even if it's only to sit in the grandstands and cheer the young champions.

Wilbur Shaw

Driver Wilbur Shaw began his first race at Indy the same year as Louis Meyer, but he had to wait until after Meyer had won three events to capture his first victory. Where Meyer was quiet and shunned the public attention showered on a three-time

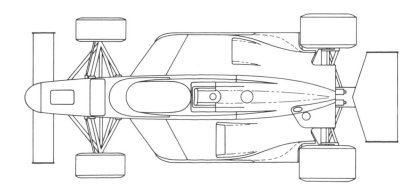

1 Low drag speedway rear wing
2 High downforce road-circuit rear wing
3 Rear bodywork
4 Engine bay cooling duct
5 Winglets
6 Radiator air outlet
7 Airscoop for turbocharger and gearbox oil cooler
8 Optional rear brake cooling duct
9 Plenum chamber
10 Boost pressure control valve
11 Refueling inlet blanking plate. Valve may be fitted to left or right side
12 Fuel vent. Tank capacity 40 U.S. gallons
13 Radio
14 Engine water radiator
15 Rearview mirror
16 Quick release steering wheel
17 Reinforced anti-intrusion cockpit surround
18 Carbon fiber monocoque top, bonded to aluminum honeycomb lower tub
19 Access cover to front coil spring-damper unit
20 Right hand coil spring-damper unit
21 Access to accelerator, clutch and brake pedals
22 Road circuit front wing
23 Speedway front wing
24 Carbon fiber nose molding
25 Strengthened nose box
26 Brake and clutch master cylinder reservoirs
27 Fire extinguisher
28 Right front air jack
29 Front ventilated disc brake and caliper
30 Front suspension upper and lower wishbones and pull-rod
31 Right hand sidepod and radiator duct
32 Gear shift linkage
33 Underwing and sidepod support
34 Radiator stone guard
35 Engine oil cooler
36 Lucas capacitor discharge ignition system
37 Mechanical fuel pump and filter
38 Cosworth DFX Turbo engine 2.65 liters, 161 cubic inches

39 Turbo intake
40 Turbocharger
41 Rear suspension rocker arm
42 Rear suspension lower wishbone
43 Rear ventilated disc brake and caliper
44 Rear coil spring-damper unit
45 Rear air jack
46 March five-speed and reverse gearbox
47 Rear wing pillar
48 Gearbox fairing
49 Right hand sidepod and oil cooler duct
50 Two-piece carbon fiber honeycomb underwing

Marlboro/Patrick March 86C

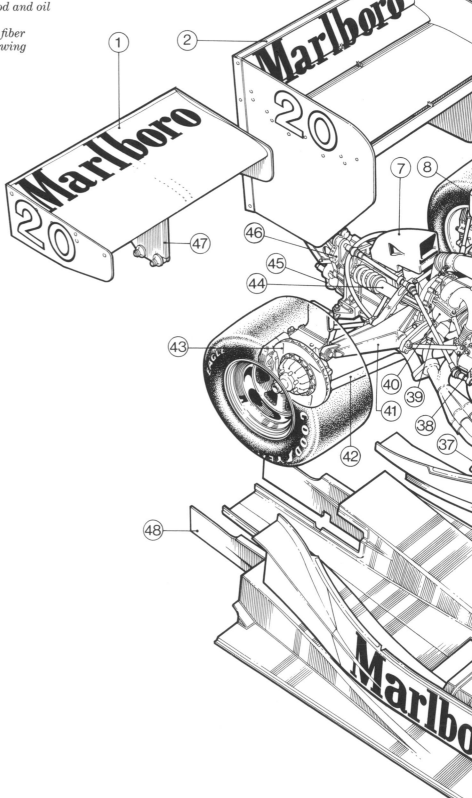

220

This illustration shows the parts of a 1986 Indy car. It depicts the March chassis and Cosworth engine of the Patrick Racing team, which was driven by Emerson Fittipaldi and sponsored by Marlboro.

winner, the fiery Shaw reveled in it. He was a master showman and had sound business judgment as well, becoming the second man to win three Indy 500 titles.

Shaw needed every bit of driving skill he possessed to win in 1937. He was leading the second-place car by two minutes in the last stages of the race when suddenly his oil-pressure gauge began to drop in each turn, showing that he was dangerously low on oil. He could return to the pits for oil, and probably sacrifice the lead, or he could drive on and risk damaging the engine when the oil ran out altogether. Shaw, who had worked on engines, decided to slow down. Not only did this lessen the strain on the engine, but it also allowed Ralph Hepburn, running second, to catch up.

With just four laps to go, Shaw was still in front, but Hepburn was just a straightaway behind him. Shaw permitted Hepburn to gain even more ground, and the cars were together coming out of Turn Four on the final lap. Then, for the first time in thirty laps, Wilbur opened the throttle. The pair thundered toward the finish line in front of the grandstand. Shaw held off Hepburn, nosing out his rival by a mere two seconds.

In 1939 Shaw dueled with Meyer for the finish. That year, Wilbur entered a new Maserati. The car was everything a driver could want. Big and fast, it handled beautifully thanks to its torsion-bar suspension, a novelty at the time. In the early going, Shaw challenged Meyer for first place until an accident erupted on Turn Two. In a chain-reaction crash, Floyd Roberts cartwheeled over the outer wall, becoming the first 500 winner to die at the Speedway.

The battle between Shaw and Meyer continued. Meyer spun once, but kept going. Then, near the end of the race, Meyer slammed into the outside wall hard and returned to the pits. With his fiercest competitor out of the race, Shaw sped on to victory. His Maserati was the first foreign-built car to win since Howdy Wilcox had captured the 1919 event in a Peugeot.

Shaw and his Maserati were back in 1940. He staved off four other drivers to take the lead with just fifty laps to go. Driver Mauri Rose had just refueled and come back into the track to challenge Shaw once more when a rainstorm began. Shaw cruised the remaining laps under the yellow flag at about 100 mph to become the first driver to win two consecutive races.

All-Time Leader

Wartime shortages of steel and fuel halted racing at the Speedway. Through the war years, Gasoline Alley sat empty and deserted. Even the exuberance spawned by the Allied victory wasn't enough to revive the cherished traditions of Indianapolis. And though Wilbur Shaw was no longer at the controls of a race car, he took great pride in assuming the reins at the Speedway. As president of the Speedway, he had more to do with bringing Indianapolis back to life than any one other person with the exception of the late owner, Tony Hulman.

At the first post-war race, in 1946, Firestone sponsored an antique car parade at the track, and I was asked to do the commentary over the public-address system. Wilbur heard my commentary and asked me to work the public-address system at the track. Thankfully, he didn't ask if I knew anything about auto racing.

Wilbur ruled the track wisely, but firmly, until his death in an airplane crash in 1954. He had a number of superstitions about racing that were law at Indianapolis. One was that a green race car was bad luck. Another was that peanuts should never be eaten in the pits. I've been known to consume many bags of peanuts at the track, but never where Wilbur could see me.

Janet Guthrie

It's too bad Wilbur didn't live long enough to know the only woman to drive at Indianapolis. His good-natured manner and flair for the dramatic could only have added to the intense publicity surrounding Janet Guthrie's race in 1978.

Arriving in Gasoline Alley for the first time in 1976, the tall, slim brunette from New York City found herself hounded by photographers every step of the way. Undaunted, she was in complete command as she worked her car to perfection. Driving a rebuilt Vollstedt-Offy, she passed her rookie driver's test easily. But owner Rolla Vollstedt readily admitted that the car simply wasn't up to the qualifying speeds and withdrew the machine before qualification trials. A.J. Foyt offered to let Guthrie qualify his spare car. During test runs, she quickly worked up to speeds of better than 181 mph, fast enough to make the starting grid. But at the last minute Foyt decided not to enter the spare car because he didn't have the pit crew necessary to service two cars in the race. Despite this disappointment at Indy, Janet became the first woman to drive at a NASCAR superspeedway, the World 600 held in Charlotte, later in the same season, and then went on to be the first woman to race in a 500-mile Indy-car event when she ran the Pocono 500.

Janet returned to Indianapolis the following year with a Wildcat chassis, but she ran into trouble early in practice. Just after she'd hit 191 mph, she lost control coming off Turn Two and rammed the outer wall. Unhurt, she described the cause of the crash simply: "I just plain lost it." The Wildcat was repaired and Janet reappeared on the final day of qualifying. Each lap of her time trial was faster than the previous, and at the end of ten miles, she owned an impressive average of 188.975 mph.

Race day, however, was disheartening. Janet was forced to the pits by an engine problem after just fifteen laps. She spent two minutes in the pits, then went back out for a single lap and came back to the pits for another twenty-three minutes. She finished the race in twenty-ninth position.

With a new car and a new sponsor, 1978 promised to hold better results for the feisty female racer. She qualified fifteenth overall and completed 190 laps to finish in ninth place. Quite a respectable showing for the month's work! Guthrie made the starting field again in 1979, but an engine malfunction forced her to quit after just three laps. Without a sponsor, Janet hasn't been back to Indianapolis since. But in four short years, she demonstrated that she was quite fit to compete with the best race drivers in the world.

Year	Winner	Year	Winner
1911	Ray Harroun	1952	Troy Ruttman
1912	Joe Dawson	1953	Bill Vukovich
1913	Jules Goux	1954	Bill Vukovich
1914	René Thomas	1955	Bob Sweikert
1915	Ralph DePalma	1956	Pat Flaherty
1916	Dario Resta	1957	Sam Hanks
1919	Howdy Wilcox	1958	Jim Bryan
1920	Gaston Chevrolet	1959	Rodger Ward
1921	Tommy Milton	1960	Jim Rathmann
1922	Jimmy Murphy	1961	A. J. Foyt, Jr.
1923	Tommy Milton	1962	Rodger Ward
1924	L. L. Corum & Joe Boyer	1963	Parnelli Jones
1925	Peter DePaolo	1964	A. J. Foyt, Jr.
1926	Frank Lockhart	1965	Jim Clark
1927	George Souders	1966	Graham Hill
1928	Louis Meyer	1967	A. J. Foyt, Jr.
1929	Ray Keech	1968	Bobby Unser
1930	Billy Arnold	1969	Mario Andretti
1931	Louis Schneider	1970	Al Unser Sr.
1932	Fred Frame	1971	Al Unser Sr.
1933	Louis Meyer	1972	Mark Donohue
1934	William Cummings	1973	Gordon Johncock
1935	Kelly Petillo	1974	Johnny Rutherford
1936	Louis Meyer	1975	Bobby Unser
1937	Wilbur Shaw	1976	Johnny Rutherford
1938	Floyd Roberts	1977	A. J. Foyt, Jr.
1939	Wilbur Shaw	1978	Al Unser Sr.
1940	Wilbur Shaw	1979	Rick Mears
1941	Floyd Davis & Mauri Rose	1980	Johnny Rutherford
1946	George Robson	1981	Bobby Unser
1947	Mauri Rose	1982	Gordon Johncock
1948	Mauri Rose	1983	Tom Sneva
1949	Bill Holland	1984	Rick Mears
1950	Johnny Parsons	1985	Danny Sullivan
1951	Lee Wallard	1986	Bobby Rahal

They also serve who stand and worry. Wrapped in multiple layers of flame-proof clothing against the extreme danger of a fuel fire in the pits, ears blocked against the constant, debilitating shriek of racing engines at full power, a pit crewman has nothing to do for most of the race . . . except worry about what can go wrong during his car's next pit stop.

He could cost the car critical seconds by fumbling a hub-nut during a tire change.

He could strip the threads on an axle-stub and put the car out of the race altogether.

He could spill raw methanol fuel on the broiling-hot engine compartment, causing a deadly fire. . . .

Nothing to do, nothing at all to do . . . except worry.

Indy cars carry forty gallons of fuel—enough for about seventy-two miles at racing speed.

Allowing for fuel-conserving caution periods, when most cars come into the pits automatically to top up their fuel tanks, this means there will be an absolute minimum of seven pit stops in the race . . . and during these frenzied seconds, the 500 can be won or lost.

The car must be refueled, tires changed and tiny, critical adjustments made to the chassis—all in not much more than eleven seconds.

An Indy car traveling at 220 mph covers 322 feet, more than a football field, every second. In even the quickest eleven-second pit stop, a car loses the length of the entire 3,330-foot front straightaway to the opposition. At Indy, speed in the pits is the essence of success . . .

In the 1986 race, despite having a car that was just as fast as the leaders, Michael Andretti (right, seen pitting in 1985) twice guessed wrong and pitted only laps before a caution light slowed the field. It cost him nearly a full lap and all hope of winning.

In 1982 Rick Mears (overleaf) got a good late-race pit stop, waves of searing heat rising from his engine cover, yet just a fraction of a second less in the pits might have made all the difference. He lost to Gordon Johncock (second overleaf) by only 0.16 of a second.

But no, in pits stops accuracy is the essence of success.

Accomplishing everything correctly and safely is a matter of life and death. A tire-changer must be perfectly certain the car's wheel nuts are fastened securely.

No, in the pits luck is everything . . . luck and timing. Knowing—or guessing—just when to come into the pits.

Early in the 1985 race, Mario Andretti's Lola, very much a contender for the win, comes into the pits. A crewman holds out a sign shaped like a long-handled ping-pong paddle, indicating exactly where Andretti must stop in order to line up with his replacement tires. The crew swarms over the car immediately—the rules allow only five workers over the wall for each car.

Air-jacks built into the bottom of the car raise it off the tires. The right front and right rear hub nuts are loosened with high-speed impact wrenches and the old tires removed.

Simultaneously, the fuel coupling is attached to the left side of the car behind the cockpit and the narrower fuel-line breather, which prevents back-pressure in the system and allows faster fuel flow, is affixed to the top of the car behind the driver.

But sometimes things don't go smoothly. In the 1973 race, Joe Leonard (overleaf) came into the pits after ninety-one laps and had time for a long chat with crew chief Johnny Capels. Indeed, there was no rush at all. One of the hubs on his Parnelli-Offy had failed. His race was run.

Under the critical eye of the USAC official, dressed in yellow, fresh rubber is mounted on the car. The old wheels are stacked neatly out of the way. The impact wrenches are pulled back over the wall—for if a car drives over one of these pneumatic hoses, it is automatically penalized one full lap.

Finally, the car comes down off its air-jacks (right) and, engine bellowing, crewmen leaning against the wing shoving it ahead, gearbox growling as the driver finds first gear, Andretti is off again.

Time: 12.5 seconds.

Fast is fast . . . but never fast enough. Lap after lap rush by. The end of the race draws nearer.

And every pit stop means precious time, precious footage, lost on the racetrack. Gordon Johncock (left) waits impatiently for his pit chief to signal him that the work—the infernally, damnably slow work—is finished.

No, not yet, Gordy. Not yet. Wait for my signal. . . .

Up the pit lane, another crew guides its driver into his pit, directs him forward, halts him abruptly at the right spot. The work begins anew —fuel in, wheels off, new wheels on. A little more front wing. Down off the jacks . . . keep the engine running—keep it running!

Back in Johncock's pit there is a violent whine. The engine revs wildly. Blue clouds of tire smoke peel off the wheels as the car streaks away, jittering and lurching over the bumpy seams of the concrete pit lane.

Meanwhile Mario Andretti's pit crew (bottom) heaves mightily against the car's rear wing. Andretti's engine matches the whine of Johncock's. The two race out of the pits together, Andretti trailing Johncock by mere feet. The crowd is on its feet, wondering which of the two will be ahead the next time they pass.

Emphasis Safety

ow do you protect a driver from injury when his racing machine slams into a concrete wall at more than 200 mph? In the old days, you couldn't but now it's beginning to seem possible. For the last few seasons, the thought of a fatality on the racetrack really hasn't entered my mind.

It hasn't always been that way. The first Indianapolis race in 1909 claimed the lives of three competitors and two spectators, and fatalities averaged one per year until 1974. Since that year, dramatic improvements in car design and racing technology have reduced the risks, although obviously the element of danger will always be present at such high speeds. Only one fatality has occurred on the track in recent years—Gordon Smiley in 1982—even though qualifying times have increased by 25 mph.

I am convinced that race fans do not attend hoping to see crashes. A fast, clean race brings cheers. The announcement of death is met with complete silence. It's a sobering moment, and though many crashes from which drivers walked away have slipped my mind, I remember vividly every detail of every crash in which a driver died. Time does not erase such memories, it merely softens the shock.

The narrow track, high speeds and sometimes poor road conditions increase the odds that a collision can happen suddenly and without warning. While the driver concentrates on the course, his machine and his opponents, he is always alert to potential danger and poised to react instantly. But being prepared sometimes isn't enough.

High Speeds, High Risks

My first experiences with the stark reality of death on the course came in 1947. Forty laps into the race, Bill Holland had the lead, followed by teammate Mauri Rose. Entering the first turn, Holland began a slide toward the grass of the infield. The velocity of the slide increased and, as he hit the dirt, the car whipped sideways, turned the other way and headed back onto the track. At that moment, William (Shorty) Cantlon, a veteran of eleven Indianapolis starts, headed into the turn. Cantlon tried to dodge Holland but he spun, hitting the wall head on. The machine rebounded, slammed the wall tail first and finally stopped against the wall in clear view of the main-stretch spectators. Shorty died instantly. Meanwhile, Holland had regained control and continued to a second-place finish behind Mauri Rose.

Though I've said the words many times, it's still difficult to announce to the crowd, "Ladies and gentlemen, it is with sincerest regret that we announce the death of . . ."

Eight years after Shorty's crash, I watched Bill Vukovich, another experienced driver, lose his life in a four-car pileup. Vukovich was a driver who liked to push his machine to its limit in every race. He had arrived at the Speedway in 1952 from Fresno, California, with solid experience in midget competition on the West Coast. Vukie got a shot at the Indy 500 the next year driving Howard Keck's new roadster. Vukie maneuvered his machine masterfully, taking a considerable lead with just nine laps to go. Suddenly the steering gave way, and the car slammed against the wall going into Turn Four. Miraculously, Vukie emerged from the crash unhurt; the crowd applauded his good fortune and consoled him on his hard luck.

Vukie was never one to enjoy attention, even when he deserved it. Undoubtedly one of the most skilled Indianapolis drivers of his era, he shunned all publicity. The first glimpse of autograph seekers sent him scurrying into the garage. Only his fellow drivers got to know him well. Few reporters were granted interviews, and his sense of humor remained hidden from the media, although he loved to needle fellow drivers, enjoyed their companionship and earned their respect as an aggressive and talented driver. The personal side of Vukie never got reported, because after being shunned a number of times, many of us felt it was better to respect his privacy.

Vukie's 1952 crash didn't seem to affect his confidence the next year. He earned the pole position and went on to win his first 500. The "Fresno Flash," as he came to be known, performed brilliantly, leading for 195 of the 200 laps. In 1954 Vukie started farther back in the pack—nineteenth position—but went on for his second Indy victory and set a new average speed of over 130 mph.

With two Indianapolis victories in three starts, Vukovich was heavily favored coming into the 1955 Indianapolis race. He qualified at over 141 mph, earning him the fifth position on the starting grid. Placing in the second row was no disadvantage to a driver as talented as Vukovich.

From my booth located near the outside of the main stretch, I could see Vukie reaching the 100-mile mark. He had a commanding lead. Suddenly the yellow light flashed on. From a point midway down the back stretch, I spotted puffs of thick black smoke rising over the track. As the field slowed, we took an inventory of the cars: Vukovich, Rodger Ward, Al Keller and Johnny Boyd were missing. Ward, Keller and Johnny Boyd survived. Vukie didn't. Although I tried to get the details from the others, they were so shaken by the pileup they wouldn't talk. It wasn't until several days later that I got a first-hand look at the accident. The films showed Rodger Ward having trouble in Turn Two. His car hit the outside wall, looped and hit the wall again. As he skidded toward the middle of the track, Johnny Boyd and Vukovich were coming out of the turn. Al Keller was in front of them. Keller headed toward the infield but spun back on the track and smashed into Boyd. Seconds later, Vukovich also slammed into Boyd, with such impact that it hurled his car over the outside wall. The machine flipped end over end half a dozen times and then burst into flames. Vukovich didn't have a chance.

Words to the Wise

Over the years, at each drivers' meeting before the Indy 500, men such as Wilbur Shaw, the late Tony Hulman, Joe Cloutier and the chief stewards have reminded the drivers of the hazards of auto racing. Though their pleas are expressed differently, it amounts to this: "You can't win the race on the first lap. Take it easy."

All drivers respect the safety rules. But when the competition is fierce and the adrenalin is flowing, some drivers briefly lose sight of those sensible instructions. It is during those brief moments that catastrophe is likely to occur, as it did in the 1958 Indy race.

Dick Rathmann and Ed Elisian had battled all month to set new speed records. Elisian set a one-lap qualifying record and started alongside Rathmann, who had set a new track record and won the pole position. The pair was running wheel-to-wheel going into Turn Three of the first lap. Elisian got into the turn first, but his tires lost traction and the rear of the car swung toward the outside wall. Rathmann tried to slip past the swerving car; there wasn't enough room. Elisian sideswiped Rathmann and both cars crashed against the wall. Close behind, Jimmy Reece slammed his brakes. Bob Veith rammed him, knocking Reece toward Pat O'Connor, who was approaching from behind. Then O'Connor's machine climbed over Reece's back right tire, flipped over and rolled to an upright position at the center of the turn. In the crashes that followed, Jerry Unser's car vaulted the wall.

Eight race cars were damaged too badly to continue. Nine others required repairs in the pit area before returning to the race. As for personal injuries, Unser suffered only shoulder injuries. Others had the expected cuts and bruises. Indiana native Pat O'Connor wasn't so lucky. He was killed. The words keep coming back to me: "You can't win the race on the first lap."

Tragedy can strike at any turn, on any lap. In the 1964 race, Dave MacDonald lost control in the fourth turn and slid into the inside wall. The fuel

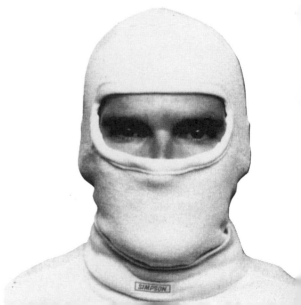

tank ruptured, engulfing the car in flames. Black smoke billowed from the car as it rebounded off the wall and into the path of Eddie Sachs. Eddie tried to avert the fireball by heading toward the high side of the track. But there was no escape. Sachs plowed broadside into the exploding machine. When the smoke thinned, Sachs and MacDonald were dead. The race was delayed for nearly two hours while the track was cleared, and when the competition resumed, only twenty-six cars remained.

At moments like that, I've often wondered how the survivors find the courage to climb back into their cars, let alone race. When asked, they just shrug if off, they feel "it won't happen to me."

Fuel of the Future

Both Sachs's and MacDonald's cars contained seventy-five gallons of gasoline. It is no wonder that the flames, which quickly reached forty feet into the air, were so difficult to bring under control. What's more, the thick black smoke obscured the drivers' views as they searched for an escape path. Shortly after the race, USAC officials banned the use of gasoline at all USAC-sponsored races. Today's competition-race cars are fueled with alcohol-based methanol. Methanol burns with a transparent flame and no smoke. It has a higher flash point, so it's less apt to ignite if spilled on a hot engine. Also, methanol contains only half the energy per gallon as gasoline. As a result, engines run cooler and more reliably. And with fewer engines coming apart, racetracks are cleaner and safer.

Methanol evaporates quickly. This characteristic helped prevent what could have been a major tragedy in 1973. Seconds after starter Pat Vidan waved the green flag, a fiery accident erupted. Driver Salt Walther, starting in the middle of the sixth row, slammed into the outside wall, fracturing his car's fuel tank. The machine traveled some 120 feet in the air before stopping upside down at the end of the main stretch. During that wild ride, fuel sprayed into the grandstands. Eleven spectators were injured and nine others had to be hospitalized

with severe burns. Had the fuel been gasoline, it could have been a holocaust. Bad as it was, most of the seventy-five gallons of methanol contained in Walther's machine had evaporated before reaching the grandstands. Walther spent most of the summer hospitalized for treatment of burns.

Fuel capacity on board the Indianapolis machines was limited to forty gallons the next year, but that was just a short-term solution. Drivers needed more protection during fiery crashes. Enter Goodyear Tire and Rubber Company.

During the Vietnam War, Goodyear had developed a helicopter fuel cell that would not fracture and burst into flame in a crash. Made of thirty-gauge gum rubber and two plies of twenty-four-ounce, rubber-impregnated nylon fabric, the new cell was virtually rupture-proof. This new technology, first adapted to race cars in 1974, has helped minimize engine fires at Indianapolis. The forty-gallon fuel cell now rides behind the driver, protected in his tub, and the engine. Moreover, the fuel cell is equipped with drybreak fittings—cut-off valves that automatically snap shut if a line is broken, preventing fuel spills.

Rear-mounted Engines

The introduction of cars with engines mounted behind the driver brought another major contribution to safer racing. But it took many years for this engineering feat to gain acceptance within the racing community.

The 1950s and early 1960s were the era of the front-engine Offenhauser-powered roadster. In its time, this machine was a vast improvement over the upright dirt-track car of the past. More streamlined and boasting better handling characteristics, this solid-axle roadster dominated Victory Lane. Roadsters designed and built by Frank Kurtis, A.J. Watson and Floyd Travis were almost look-alikes. Driver-designer Jack Brabham started the rear-engine revolution at Indy in 1961. Two years later, Colin Chapman's Team Lotus secured the rear-engine's place in history, when Jim Clark finished a

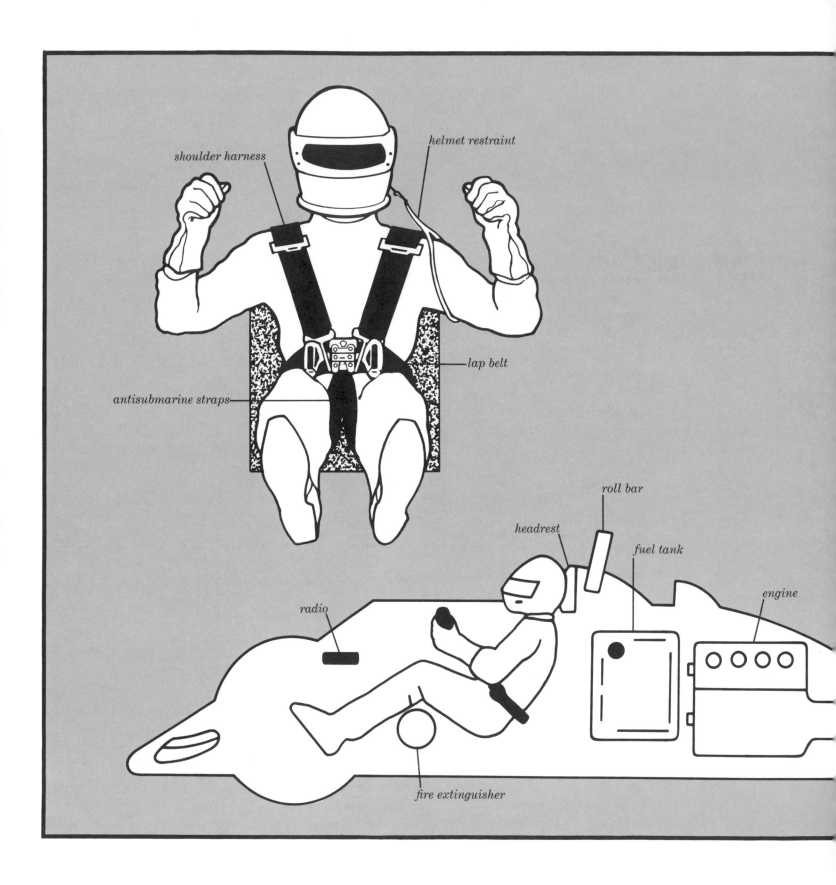

shoulder harness

helmet restraint

antisubmarine straps

lap belt

roll bar

headrest

fuel tank

engine

radio

fire extinguisher

244

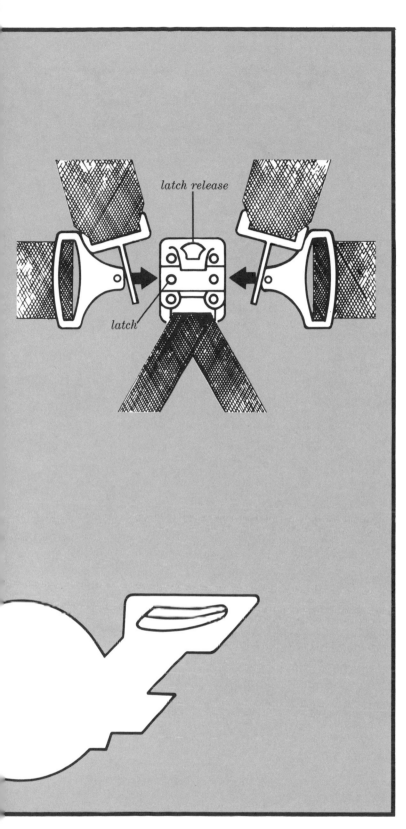

latch release

latch

To keep the driver from being thrown out of the car, a safety harness consisting of shoulder straps, lap belt and antisubmarine straps ties him into the tub. The helmet restraint is attached at the left side of the helmet and loops over the left arm.

promising second—and everyone knew the front-engine roadster's days were numbered. Team after team converted to the new rear-engine cars, but their reasoning was simply that the new machines were faster. Few were convinced that they were far safer than the roadsters. In fact, many Speedway regulars felt the rear-engine cars were too light, that they weren't as substantial or as sturdy as the front-engine roadsters. It took a while to convince them that they were actually safer.

I have vivid memories of roadsters that crashed, killing the driver but doing little visual damage to the vehicle. In a roadster, the driver absorbs eighty percent of the shock of a crash, the car only twenty percent. It is just the reverse in a rear-engine machine because the driver sits in a capsule of aluminum and carbon fiber called the "tub." During a crash, the suspension system absorbs the initial shock. Often the frame and engine separate, while the tub withstands shock after shock—and the driver survives.

Danny Ongais's experience in 1981 serves as a good example. A shy, quiet guy, Danny is fully capable of running a first-class operation. Danny managed the Interscope team for several seasons, with financial backing from Ted Fields. Away from the track one day, Danny told me he'd like to see all speed restrictions eliminated at the Speedway. "Bring what you're big enough to drive," he said. That's certainly one form of courage!

Ongais was leading the 1981 race, but a glacially slow forty-six-second-long pit stop had him roaring out of the pits to make up lost time, leaving a long black strip of rubber. He never completed the lap. Entering Turn Three, the car suddenly veered to the outside wall, crashed and then continued at a three-quarter angle around the wall. Parts were flying in all directions. When the machine stopped, the front end was gone. After four days in intensive care at Methodist Hospital in Indianapolis, Ongais was flown to a Los Angeles hospital, where he completed his recovery.

Writer-driver Patrick Bedard can also verify the

245

strength of the tub. In the 1984 race, going into Turn Three, Bedard's car went out of control and rammed the infield bank. It hit with such force that the car disintegrated on impact, hurling debris in every direction. The machine flipped end over end down the track, and the cockpit came to rest upside down in the grass. How could any driver survive? It looked impossible.

This was exactly the same kind of accident—end-over-end flip—that had killed Bill Vukovich three decades earlier. The advances in safer car design saved Bedard. And although he suffered a broken jaw and severe concussion, Bedard was still able to address guests at the victory banquet via a television hookup from his hospital bed.

Better Built Cars

Significant improvements to the tub have been made since 1981, particularly the introduction of carbon fiber. The lower half of the tub, which sits in the main chassis, is made of aluminum-honeycomb laminate (two strong sheets of aluminum molded with a honeycomb of aluminum between). The upper half of the tub is composed of carbon fiber, which looks like black fiberglass. Though one-fourth the weight of aluminum, it is far stronger.

When Rick Mears, Derek Daly and Kevin Cogan all suffered serious leg injuries during the 1985 season, USAC officials responded immediately by calling for a new front-end design. The new cars have a foot box that incorporates the clutch and master-brake cylinders within the chassis. These must be spaced at least six inches away from a new, added bulkhead. Hopefully, this added length will eliminate leg injuries.

Protective Armor

Made of several layers of fiberglass with a polystyrene liner, the driver's helmet is hard, but not as hard as it could be. Unlike the tub built to withstand shocks, the shell and liner will crush in a crash, absorbing the force of the impact and sparing the driver's head. It does not, however, spare the

helmet; after one crash, it's damaged beyond repair. The cost? About $1,000 per helmet.

Beyond their safety function, helmets are very much a part of a team's identity. Drivers have them decorated to coordinate with the team's colors. Memorizing the color schemes of the individual drivers is the one certain method of knowing who's actually in a machine, inasmuch as only a driver's head is visible in the cockpit.

From the announcing booth, I can tell instantly from the helmet who's driving a car. Johnny Rutherford's helmet is red, white and blue with a big star on it—the Lone Star of Texas. Foyt's helmet is a color I call "Foyt orange" with his initials "A.J." on the sides. Mario Andretti's helmet is red and silver, while Emerson Fittipaldi's is a weblike pattern of fluorescent orange and bright blue.

To protect the body, every driver wears a flame-retardant suit, usually made of Nomex, manufactured by Du Pont. The coveralls, the gloves —even the underwear—are made of Nomex. Three layers of fabric are quilted together with Nomex thread to create the best possible protection against fire. A full suit costs about $1,500.

Fire Alarm

A fire on the racetrack is one thing; fire in the pits is another. Again, modern technology is winning this battle. A car begins the race with forty gallons of methanol. The tank in the pit holds another 240 gallons. This means that a car must average 1.8 miles per gallon to complete the 500 miles. It also means there will be at least seven or eight fuel stops during the race—seven or eight opportunities for spilling fuel on a hot race car.

It's happened. Rick Mears and several of his crew members were severely burned in 1981 and his car destroyed when fuel was spilled on the engine during a stop. Since then, race officials have introduced a new fueling system. With the new machinery, fuel can't be released until the nozzle is perfectly connected inside the car's fuel cell. Fewer spills caused by over-anxious pit men will hopefully

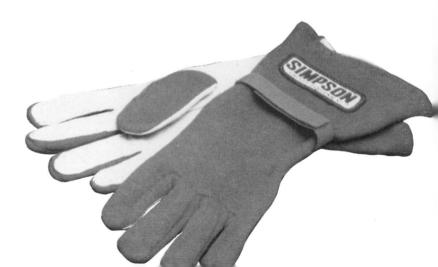

result in fewer fires in the pit areas.

When a fire does break out in the pits or on the track, there are three hundred firemen ready for action. Four firemen are assigned to each car's pit area, with the remainder stationed around the track. I've often watched in admiration as these men rush to an accident seemingly unmindful of their own safety, artfully dodging the race traffic. Water is the most effective weapon against an alcohol fire, and a mammoth six-inch water line with outlets at every other pit has been installed. This system could literally flood the pit area in seconds.

In addition to a dedicated team of fire fighters, more than two hundred medical personnel are on site each day of the race. The infield hospital is equipped to handle any emergency.

The British Are Coming

Over the years, many car builders have debuted their designs at the Indy 500. The Coyote, Wildcat, Penske, Eagle, Chaparral, Lola and March have all visited Victory Lane. In the mid-1980s, however, only three chassis builders remain—Lola, March and Eagle. Roger Penske is hoping to change this hegemony with a new Anglo-American car, introduced in 1986. But although the Penske PC-15 is American-owned, like the Lola and March it is built in England.

Of the major chassis builders, the English companies Lola and March dominate. The Lola firm, located in Cambridgeshire, was the first to arrive at Indy; in 1966 Graham Hill drove a Lola to victory. The same year another Lola, driven by Jackie Stewart, led after 190 laps, but the engine blew and the car finished sixth. Lola was absent in 1967 and 1968, returning three years later when driver Mark Donohue finished seventh. The next Indianapolis victory came in 1978, when Al Unser Sr. won in a Lola. The builder wasn't represented again until 1983; Mario Andretti of the Newman/Haas team drove a Lola T-700 chassis.

Since 1969 March Engineering of Oxfordshire, England, has had success in all types of Formula competition, building winning Formula One, Two and Three cars. But the first March didn't appear at Indianapolis until 1981. Tom Sneva drove one of three March chassis entered that year. Sneva won the battle for the pole, convincing other owners that the March was a fast, reliable chassis. The next year there were seventeen March cars in the field. But the moment of truth came in 1983, when Tom Sneva won the Indy 500 in a March, setting a pattern of March victories for years to come.

On a windy April day in Gasoline Alley, I asked Robin Herd, the tall, intelligent Englishman who heads up March Engineering, why the English car builders dominate the field. Robin flashed a smile and replied: "I think everything runs in cycles. If you Americans can put a man on the moon, surely you can succeed in building a race car."

Herd's background is in aeronautics; not surprisingly, March applied aeronautical test procedures to race cars. Herd assured me that, for his company, safety is job one. "When any designer designs a car, the factor foremost in his mind is safety. We took three cars and destroyed them at an aeronautical center in Britain. By mounting high-speed cameras, we could learn the effect on the driver. We are still a long way from where we can get to. We try to build a 'survival cell' around the driver. People are going to go on racing, and we've got to make it acceptably safe."

Although two American-built cars were in the 1985 starting field, both Eagle chassis owned and built by Dan Gurney and driven by Tom Sneva and Ed Pimm, none made the 1986 race. Gurney's newest Eagle just wasn't fast enough to qualify. Dan Gurney has been racing and building cars for more than twenty-five years and he has two second-place finishes at Indy. His Eagle chassis have won Indianapolis three times, twice with Bobby Unser driving and once with Gordon Johncock at the wheel. Dan was instrumental in encouraging Colin Chapman and Lotus to bring their designs to the Speedway. Many people believe Dan will someday build an Eagle that will run faster than a March.

Safety Zone

Since 1911 race-car building has developed into a science. And along the way, the lessons learned on the racetrack have been applied to the design of passenger cars. Indy's first winner, Ray Harroun, is credited with using the first rearview mirror. While most of the other drivers had a mechanic riding with them who could spot approaching cars, Harroun drove alone and needed a mirror to see the vehicles behind him. (Locally, Ray was equally well-known for having been married seven times!)

Prior to World War I, automobile manufacturers did not own test grounds as they do today, and they looked to the Speedway to discover solutions for mechanical and design problems. Four-wheel brakes and hydraulic shock absorbers, low-pressure (balloon) tires, better tire compounds, and of course seat belts were all used at Indianapolis long before they became standard equipment for passenger cars. In recent years, the Speedway engineers have placed more emphasis on improved suspension systems, more efficient shock absorbers, fuel injection, turbocharged engines, disc brakes and still better tires. Although turbocharged engines have been around for many years, the new popularity of turbo passenger cars surely can be attributed to the tryouts at Indy.

As long as automobile manufacturers remain attuned to innovations at the Speedway, passenger cars will undoubtedly become safer. The drivers who routinely walk away from 200-mph crashes have much to teach automobile manufacturers—it's just a question of time and a willingness to listen.

Racing is dangerous. There isn't a professional racing driver on the face of the earth who doesn't know and accept it. It's simply the fact.

Yet something in the human animal—particularly if that human animal happens to be a professional racing driver—encourages it to believe, even amidst the most threatening of hazards, that all will go well; it won't happen to him.

Alas, despite consummate skill, the best equipment and the most astute preparation, occasionally "it" happens. Which is only another way of reiterating the immutable fact—racing is dangerous.

Yet year by year, with each incident, each violent brush with the infinite, valuable lessons are learned. Techniques for building race cars improve, better materials and design concepts are found.

Increasingly complex rules are written that require more effective minimum-safety standards.

When Danny Ongais had a horrendous crash in 1981 (right), the safety crews were on the spot immediately. In a life-threatening incident—and absolutely every crash at Indianapolis is treated as life-threatening until it is proven otherwise—the yellow light flashes on instantly to slow the race cars. Without a second's hesitation, the safety crews race to the scene, leap from the trucks, go to work. Fire is put out. The driver is protected.

In Ongais's case, he suffered badly broken feet and legs, requiring a year of painful recuperation. In following years, car construction rules were rewritten to require improved foot protection for the driver—as the direct result of mishaps like this one.

Moving at greater velocity than the take-off speed of a commercial jetliner, the car begins to rotate. Their angle of attack now reversed, the car's wings begin generating vertical thrust instead of downforce. The car is lifted on the air.

Rising, hurtling like a great blue marlin on the hook, it tumbles madly.

In a blinding flash of flame, it impacts the concrete outside wall. The intake manifold flies away. Ruptured fuel tanks vent raw methanol. The disintegrating car is bathed in leaping clouds of fire.

Still moving at over 150 mph, it somersaults forward, cartwheeling over its nose. The gearbox and rear wheels separate from the car and the rear wing careens down the track, a torn piece of scrap aluminum.

The car rises again on the air, burning fuel trailing out behind. Spectators viewing from the Turn-Two luxury suites beyond the fence retreat in horror, protecting their faces from the flames' intense heat.

Once more the car comes to earth. This time it lands with such violence that the four-cylinder Offy engine is torn from its mounts. The engine careens down the track alone, a lethal bundle seeking targets of its own.

Only torn connectors and parted cables hang off behind the driver's compartment now. Two pieces of screen used to protect the car's dual radiators fly free.

Sliding, twisting, spinning, the car grinds along the track surface. Wispy vapors of flame still rise on the air as it spins onward. The engine tumbles past, end over end. The speed is ebbing now.

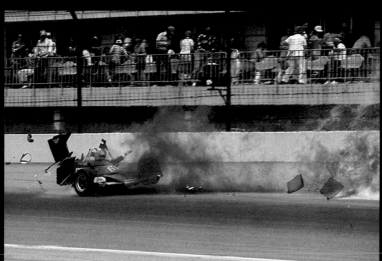

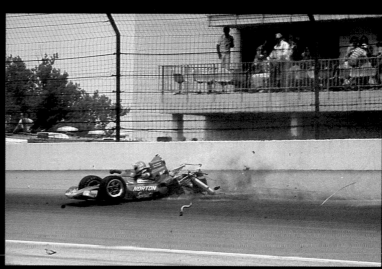

Finally, it is over. The engine rests at the side of the track. Ten feet away, the driver slumps forward over the wheel, his blue helmet an indistinguishable component of the wreckage.

Incredibly, Tom Sneva emerged from his horrific 1975 crash with only minor injuries. Yet this accident, together with many others, encouraged designers to find better ways of isolating race-car fuel systems.

In succeeding years, Goodyear developed extremely tough, crash-resistant fuel cells. The rules were changed to require location of the tanks away from the car's crash-vulnerable perimeters. Finally, effective dry-break fuel couplings, which seal automatically when ruptured, have greatly reduced the dangers of fire in Indy-car crashes.

But racing crashes are still inevitable. In 1973 Johnny Parsons Jr. and Mario Andretti tangled in the south chute (overleaf), Parsons sliding off the track with broken front suspension, while Al Unser Sr. (yellow car) runs over Parsons's shattered front wing. Andretti careens out of control several hundred yards ahead.

Neither driver was hurt, but the safety workers were on the scene immediately.

During the caution period while the wrecked cars are cleared away, the remaining racers form a line behind the pace car (overleaf, lower right), allowing room for emergency vehicles to maneuver safely on the track.

In the pits there is an odd, inexplicable commotion. Heat shimmers off the car as it is refueled—seems normal enough.

But suddenly men are running. One of them falls to the ground and rolls across the concrete over and over. He is yelling, gesturing at himself madly. Nothing can be seen. There is no flame.

Yet the man is on fire. Methanol is used at Indy because it is safer, far less volatile, than gasoline.

However, it has a serious shortcoming—it burns with an invisible flame. In daylight, a methanol fire may look like nothing more than heat vapor, though it is in full, raging flame.

Therefore, the Speedway fire crews take no chances. When Tom Sneva crashed in Turn One during the 1985 race (bottom and overleaf), safety crews thoroughly coated his March-Cosworth with fire extinguishant, making certain no invisible conflagration could begin.

In 1981 one of USAC's pit-fire control personnel is led away after a pit-stop methanol fire singed his shirt and pant leg (right). Quick thinking on the part of his fellow workers saved him from serious burns.

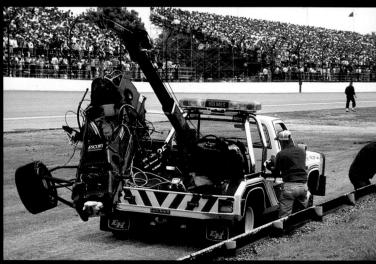

In the 1984 race, Pat Bedard suffered one of the most violent crashes in Speedway history (above). Coming through the north chute, his March-Cosworth went out of control, careened downed into the infield, caught its wheels in the soft grass and began to cartwheel wildly.

For two hundred yards, the car went end over end time after time, shedding bodywork and mechanical pieces. When it finally came to rest, nothing was left of the shattered car except the right front wheel and the cockpit undershell surrounding the driver's compartment.

Fortunately, the important fuel-cell system and dry-break fuel couplings all worked perfectly, preventing a fire, and the very sturdy March cockpit survived intact, protecting the driver from serious bone breakage.

What the car could not do, however, was protect Bedard from the infinite physical violence of being thrown at the ground again and again at extremely high speed. While his helmet saved his life, Bedard's head hit the roll-bar a ferocious blow, knocking him semiconscious and resulting in a severe

Track safety crews stand by in case of fire, while emergency medical workers remove the semiconscious Bedard from his wrecked car. He is ministered to, laid on a stretcher, wheeled to the waiting ambulance, helicoptered to the hospital

Simultaneously, track safety crews haul away the remaining bits of Bedard's racer so that the 500 can resume.

Miraculously, two weeks later Bedard was released from the hospital.

...lysm at 200 mph. ... Andretti (left) goes into the wall, his Lola's shattered fiberglass bodywork peeling back off the chassis. Johnny Parsons Jr. slides along the wall, immediately behind.

Beyond a certain point, no matter how well-engineered a race car may be, if it loses directional stability at Indy speeds, it becomes completely uncontrollable. From then on, the driver can only hang on, wait, wonder what's in store. This time, for Andretti and Parsons, fortune was generous. Neither was hurt.

Such was not the case for Andretti's Lola. Yet viewed in the Garage Area afterwards (right), the car had done its job. Its well-designed monocoque chassis had absorbed the crash's potentially lethal energy. Like the wreckage of John Paul Jr.'s 1985 March (overleaf), its racing career was over—but its driver would race another day.

Seventy-fifth Birthday

ew race-day Sundays have approached holding more promise than the 1986 Indianapolis 500: the qualifying speeds up to an astounding 217 mph, an all-star field of drivers, the cars of the major teams intact and running well, and the Speedway celebrating its seventy-fifth anniversary. The night before the race, however, trouble began. The one element that can capriciously and unpredictably prevent the 500 is rain. The lowering clouds that swept in on Saturday—the advance guard of a bubble of high-pressure creeping down from the Canadian plains—opened up Saturday night. A heavy, pelting rain drenched the course. It flooded the track and washed down the brand-new buildings in Gasoline Alley containing the thirty-three machines which had been so meticulously prepared for the morrow's fray.

Race-day morning dawned gray and wet. Indianapolis fans are eternal optimists, and not without reason. Over the years, they've won many battles with the elements. Though it was still raining when the gates opened, the faithful gathered at the park, quickly filling it to capacity.

By late morning, the rain stopped. The racecourse appeared well-drained and absent of any standing water so a parade of multi-hued pickups scurried onto the track accompanied by the pace cars and jet-powered vacuums. As the vacuums sucked water off the asphalt, the other vehicles warmed and dried the pavement with the friction of their tires.

Then the *real* parade started: The procession of vintage Indy cars in the scheduled salute to the seventy-fifth anniversary of the Indianapolis 500. The Marmon driven to victory by Ray Harroun in 1911 was first, followed by three-time winner Louis Meyer, eighty-two years old, driving the car in which he'd won the 1928 race. A. J. Foyt's winning

entry from the 1961 race was next.

The enthusiasm of the 400,000-plus crowd grew as each new machine and each former champion appeared on the track. The crowd anxiously anticipated the drop of the starter's flag. What dropped instead was more rain. The race stewards, seeing the condition of the track and the threatening appearance of the skies, postponed the race until the following morning, Monday. The teams took the machines, and their taut nerves, back to the garages. The spectators, their appetites teased by a month of celebration and the promising competition in practice, headed back to their hotels, homes or campsites to wait out the weather.

Anticipation

The crowd had every reason to expect a classic contest. Car designers and engineers had all predicted new speed records. And less than two hours into qualifying, 1985 Indianapolis winner Danny Sullivan set three new track records in the four-lap run: first lap, 215.729 mph, a new track record; second lap, 215.755 mph, another new track record. Third and fourth laps of 215.636 and 214.413 mph gave Sullivan an average of 215.382 mph, the fastest qualifying laps ever run at the Speedway. An hour later, teammate Rick Mears blazed past Sullivan's brand new records: first lap, 217.581 mph, a new track record; three more laps at better than 216 mph gave Mears an average of 216.828 mph, another new track record. That run put the brilliant yellow machine on the pole, but more importantly it signalled that Mears had recovered fully from the devastating leg injuries suffered in a 1984 crash.

Field of Fame

With Mears and Sullivan in the first row, the powerful Penske Racing team dominated the front of the field. They were joined on Row One by young Michael Andretti. Just two weeks earlier Michael had posted his first Indy-car victory at Long Beach, California.

The owner of Andretti's entry, Maurice Kraines,

started his well-financed team in 1982. The founder of Kraco Enterprises, which sells car stereo equipment, Kraines even went to race-driver's school in 1983 in order to get a first-hand understanding of the challenges faced by his drivers. But despite the millions of dollars Kraines had invested in a huge modern facility in California, the Kraco team had little early success. For the 1986 season Kraines hired skilled chief mechanic Barry Green and engineer Adrian Newey to revitalize the operation. One important decision was to cut the team down from two cars to one; another was selecting Michael Andretti as his sole driver.

Long Odds

If the Speedway gave an award for succeeding against the greatest odds, it would have gone to Phil Krueger. He'd tried to qualify at Indianapolis for five years without success; driving marginal equipment, he'd crashed three times. In 1985 Phil hired on as a mechanic for another team, but in his spare time Krueger assembled an entry from a car wrecked by Foyt at Michigan that year. He worked as builder, chief mechanic, engineer, engine rebuilder and driver, and managed to get backing from Leader Cards. Qualifying at just under 208 mph, Krueger put the only "used" car into the 1986 starting lineup, an achievement that defied all the laws of probability.

Krueger's pursuit of the starting field was impressive, but so was that of his teammate Gary Bettenhausen. Gary failed to qualify in 1983 and 1984, and didn't even have a ride in 1985. After fourteen starts at Indianapolis, Gary's hopes of winning at the Speedway were dim. In 1986 Ralph Wilkie of Leader Card Racing gave Gary a shot in a new March chassis and on the final day of qualifications, he made it onto the starting grid with an average speed of almost 210 mph. In the pits afterwards, tears flowed from Gary's eyes as he talked about his dream: "I think my brother Tony and I can appreciate this race more than anyone. This place has not been good to the Bettenhausen

family. My dad started fourteen 500s, only finished two and lost his life here in 1961. I almost had it won in 1972; I had led the most laps when my engine blew near the end. Since I was a boy, an Indy victory has been my goal. I remember hearing my dad talking about it and how much he wanted to win."

A New Day

After the disappointment of cancellation on Sunday, Monday brought no relief; it rained most of the day and the fans stayed away. Track officials decided to hold the race the following Saturday, May 31. It gave race teams and rain-weary track workers a chance to recharge their enthusiasm, and the fans an opportunity to make plans. On race day, most of the reserved seats were filled and only the infield crowd had thinned. Attendance on Saturday was still about 300,000.

From the drop of starter Duane Sweeney's flag, the race was the most competitive 500 I've ever called. Michael Andretti led the first forty-two laps with Rick Mears, Bobby Rahal and Kevin Cogan challenging. On Lap 42, Andretti pitted for fuel and a new set of tires, then pulled in again a few short laps later; the stagger was wrong on the new tires. That second stop cost Andretti the lead, but the opportunity offered by his unscheduled stop proved hard for the others to exploit.

By Lap 125, the half-way point, the lead had changed ten times. Cogan, Al Unser Jr., Emerson Fittipaldi, Mears and Rahal spelled each other in the first position. At the half-way point, Rahal was in the lead and burning up the asphalt, his average speed 13 mph above the previous track record. In four short years on the circuit, Rahal had captured the pole position ten times and won eight races, but had enjoyed little luck at Indianapolis. The pre-race publicity had focused on the incumbent champion, Sullivan, and on pole-sitter Mears, who was heavily favored to win.

With only seventy-five miles to go, Mears owned the lead, and Rahal and Cogan followed in close pursuit. Despite having set a new record in qualifying (a full

two miles per hour faster than either Rahal or Cogan), Mears's machine was not performing well in traffic. Rahal screamed by Mears coming out Turn Two and took the lead with thirteen laps remaining. Kevin Cogan began stalking the hapless second-place Mears and passed him to the outside on Turn Four. As Mears explained it, "Kevin came by me on the outside like I was tied to a post."

On Lap 187 it was Rahal-Cogan-Mears. One more trip past the start-finish line and Cogan made his move on Rahal, reached him in Turn One and poured on the speed, dashing ahead of his pursuers smartly. Now, with twelve laps remaining, Cogan had taken the lead by displaying his typical daring. The handsome Cogan, who has also worked as a male model, has run up against every kind of frustration in his five years as a championship driver. But after joining Patrick Racing at the beginning of 1986, Cogan's luck changed, and his first championship win followed in the season opener at Phoenix.

Now, leading the Indianapolis 500, Cogan looked unstoppable. He was driving brilliantly, and his car was running superbly. It looked as though even the blistering speed of Bobby Rahal wouldn't be enough to keep Cogan out of Victory Lane. But with the winners on Lap 184, Arie Luyendyk cut a tire in Turn Four and spun toward the pit entrance. The accident brought out the yellow flag and the pack slowed, allowing Rahal and Mears to close the gap on Cogan, positioning themselves for a dash to the finish. Safety crews scrambled to clear the accident. No one wants the 500 to end on a yellow flag—especially not with three top drivers wheel-to-wheel and ready to contest what looked like a walkover by Cogan.

Five Miles and a Cloud of Dust

The pace car pulled into the pits as the leaders neared the end of Lap 197, unleashing a blazing three-way, five-mile sprint to the finish. As the green flag dropped, Rahal shot up the straightaway in Cogan's draft, then swerved back down to the inside, beating Cogan into Turn One. Rahal had simply drafted past Kevin.

Rahal, leading the pack, now wondered if he could finish the race. His red low-fuel warning lamp had been flashing for a half-dozen laps. But Bobby had been a bridesmaid too many times on this track. Faced with a choice of stopping for fuel during the yellow flag and giving up his dream or going for broke, Rahal staked everything on the fumes left in his tank. Chased by Cogan and Mears, Rahal held nothing back, pushing the pace on the final lap to 209.152 mph, the fastest race lap yet recorded at Indianapolis. The four laps run under the yellow made good Rahal's gamble, saving enough fuel to take the checkered flag just 1.4 seconds ahead of Cogan and 1.8 seconds in front of Mears.

The fastest race on record, it was also the shortest 500—with an elapsed time of two hours fifty-five minutes, the first 500 run in under three hours. Rahal's average speed was 170.722 mph, beating the mark set by Mears in 1984 by more than 7 mph.

The End of the Rainbow

For Bobby Rahal, it was a short drive from the yard of bricks at the finish line to the end of a long personal quest for the Speedway's Victory Lane. It was the end of a rainbow for someone else, too. For thirteen years, Rahal had been backed by Jim Trueman, owner of the Truesports team. Rahal was like a son to the athletic Trueman, himself a noted road-racing driver and the founder of the Red Roof Inns motel chain.

In his dash for the flag, Rahal was racing more than just two formidable driving opponents. He carried with him Jim Trueman's hopes. In 1984 Trueman underwent surgery for cancer. He had responded well to chemotherapy, but early in 1986 he took a turn for the worse. Although Jim was gravely ill on race day, he was able to join Bobby and his wife, Debbie, in the pace car for a victory lap. In Victory Lane, Bobby's first words were: "This one's for Jim Trueman. This is the one thing I could give him." Trueman confided, "All I asked Bobby this morning was to do the best he could. He drove the best race of his life." Eleven days later, the fifty-two year old sportsman died.

All That Glitters

The "race of his life" earned Bobby Rahal the preeminent position at an informal dinner hosted by Mary Hulman George, vice-president of the Speedway and Tony Hulman's daughter, the following evening. He also earned $581,052.50—a record for Indianapolis. The total prize monies had grown by $750,000 in a single year to top four million dollars.

The 1986 race, though delayed a week by the rains, was the most competitive in the seventy-five-year history of the track. Three men, all champions, all with first-class equipment and with first-class teams behind them, contested the race right down to the checkered flag—without a single serious accident.

In the year 2011 the Indianapolis 500 will mark its hundredth anniversary. If the rulemakers permit the same kind of increases in speed in the next quarter century as they have in the last, the winner might well run the track at 270 mph or more. Already, designers talk of covering the fat front tires of the cars to reduce aerodynamic drag. Who knows what speeds will be possible?

One thing is certain, however. Just as generations of drivers—be it the Unsers, Bettenhausens, Andrettis, Brabhams or some as yet unknown clan—will keep their dreams set on the Indy 500, so too will generations of sports fans return to take part in this deep-rooted national celebration. More than a race, the Indy 500 is a great American tradition.

In the end, there is only winning. All else is empty prattle. No driver comes to Indianapolis just to be seen. The goal is easy to understand. You're there to prove you're the fastest. The bravest. The best. And in any year, there can be only one.

The race is nearly over. Car after car have dropped out with mechanical trouble. There have been crashes. Men have gone to the hospital.

During 500 grueling miles, car numbers have zoomed up and down the great leader board in the pit lane (overleaf), as fortune alternately smiled, frowned, smiled again. But only one moment will tell the story—the magic moment. The finish.

Ten laps to go.

Eight.

Five.

The crowd comes to its feet, stretching to see who it will be. The best, fastest, bravest is mere moments away from being unveiled.

The white flag. One more lap. After almost three hours of speed, strategy, courage, danger . . . one more lap.

And there it is! The car flashes past! Time balks at the sight— the checkered flag!

The crowd waves and howls, ecstatic at being a part of the moment. The winning car makes a final slow tour, the driver waving, fist clenched.

Finally, triumphantly, he comes down the pit lane for the last time. On this day, he's proven who's best, by God— proven it for all time.

In the post-race hysteria, thirty-two drivers pass quietly into the garages. In Victory Lane, one driver passes into history.

Danny Sullivan, 1985

As the reigning Indy 500 champion, his prize money together with the commercial endorsements that will come his way in the next twelve months will combine to make him a rich man. He will be on television morning, noon and night. They will ask him the same question again and again—what has winning Indy really meant for him?

Smiling politely, he will reply, handing back the same modest response.

This man is a millionaire. A national institution. If he never does another significant thing in his life, he will always be famous.

Bobby Rahal, 1986.

Yet what does winning Indy really mean?

Winning Indy means many things. It means having accomplished a task of extreme difficulty, and accomplishing it better than the best of one's peers.
It means becoming a member of one of racing's smallest and most exclusive fraternities—the fraternity of Indy 500 winners.

It means having survived a severe test of courage and determination in good health. It means having been part of a team which, competing against other teams with unlimited resources and technical help, proved itself the best.
Most of all, it means that on this most demanding of days, in this most demanding of races, he has publicly demonstrated one fact to which even the Fates must now grudgingly acquiesce—he's a winner.

Authors

Tom Carnegie, who wrote the text, is the voice of the Indianapolis Motor Speedway. A celebrity in the racing world, he has called every Indy 500 race since 1946. All drivers recognize his final authority when they hear his deep voice echo over the loudspeaker: "It's a new track record!" Carnegie is also a racing commentator for WRTV Indianapolis. Each year he heads the broadcast team's coverage of the track from qualifying through race day.

Patrick Bedard, writer, editor and Indy driver, contributed the foreword. For twelve years he pursued racing, from club racing in a Pinto to the international arenas of LeMans and the Indy 500. He was the first to top 200 mph at Indianapolis in a stock-block powered car (a March-Buick in 1984). Bedard has a B.S. in mechanical engineering and a master's degree in automotive engineering. He is editor-at-large of *Car and Driver*, and writes a regular column in addition to covering road tests and contributing feature stories. Other publications include *Sports Illustrated* and *Esquire*.

Ted West, author of the captions, is a sports journalist who has written about auto racing in the United States and Europe for almost twenty years. Since 1972 he has specialized in Indy coverage. West is the East Coast editor of *Road & Track* and, in the 1970s, worked at *Car and Driver* as articles editor. He has contributed to numerous sports magazines, including *Motor Trend*, *Autoweek*, *The Motor* (London) and *Hot Rod*.

Text Consultant

David Abrahamson, a magazine editor and writer, is contributing editor of *Car and Driver*, and worked for this magazine for many years as managing editor. In 1973 he was editor-in-chief of *Autoweek*. His work has appeared in a variety of publications, including *The New York Times Sunday Magazine*, *Playboy* and *Science '86*.

Contributing Photographers

The IMS Photography Staff, headed by director Ron McQueeney, keeps the official archives of the Indianapolis Motor Speedway. With over a million photographs dating from 1909 through the present, IMS has the largest documentation of the Indy 500 in the world.

Chet Jezierski, photographer, illustrator and painter, has covered the Indy-car race circuit for over ten years. His photographs have appeared in numerous magazines, and Jezierski is the photographer and author of the book *Speed! Indy Car Racing*.

Bill Stahl specializes in auto-racing. In the last seven years, in addition to his documentary photographs, he has pioneered a new type of LaserArt photography, seen on the book jacket. His photographs have appeared in many publications, including *Sports Illustrated*, *Road & Track*, *Car and Driver*, *Motor Trend*, *Automotive Year* and *Popular Photography*.

Bob Tronolone photographed his first race in 1957, and has covered the Indianapolis 500 every year since 1961. His photographs have appeared in many car and racing publications in the United States and Europe. Tronolone has also contributed to several books. For over twenty years, he has been employed by the Hughes Aircraft Company.

Glossary

CART
Championship Auto Racing Teams. An independent organization that sanctions all Indy-car races in the United States except the Indianapolis 500. Founded by Indy-car owner Roger Penske and U.E. "Pat" Patrick in 1979, CART establishes chassis and engine specifications and supervises each event.

Flag signals
The sign language to the driver via flags from the flagman. Black: pull into the pit for consultation; Blue with an orange diagonal stripe: a faster car is overtaking you, give consideration; Checkered: the race is finished; Green: start; Red: stop, unsafe conditions; White: you are entering the last lap; and Yellow: caution, slow and hold position.

Formula Ford
An open-wheel, single-seat race car with a 1600cc, stock Ford, rear engine of 90 horsepower and a chassis weighing at least 850 pounds. An entry-level race car.

Formula One car
An open-wheel, single-seat race car with a 1500cc, turbocharged rear engine with unlimited boost for over 900 horsepower and a chassis weighing 1,212 pounds. This competition series is international.

Formula Two car
A scaled-down version of the Formula One car, with a non-turbocharged 2000cc, fuel-injected rear engine of 325 horsepower and a minimum chassis weight of 1,135 pounds. The Formula Two series was discontinued in 1984.

Formula Three car
A scaled-down version of the Formula One car, with a non-turbocharged 1600cc, fuel-injected rear engine of 165 horsepower and a minimum chassis weight of 1,000 pounds.

Indy car
An open-wheel, single-seat race car with a 2650cc rear engine capable of 750 horsepower and minimum chassis weights of 1,550 pounds for turbocharged engines and 1,475 pounds for non-turbocharged engines.

INDY 500™
A registered trademark owned and used by the Indianapolis Motor Speedway Corporation in conjunction with entertainment services it renders by an annual automobile race and related events held in Speedway, Indiana.

Midget car
A small, solid-axle, open-wheel, single-seat race car with a wheelbase of at least 66 inches and no more than 76 inches, a front engine capable of 200 horsepower, and an average chassis weight of 800 pounds.

NASCAR
National Association of Stock Car Racing. The governing body of major stock-car racing in the United States.

Off-road racing
Supervised competition in stock-car classes, involving assorted vehicles that are designed with a high ride to handle rough terrain.

Oval track
A closed course with a dirt or asphalt surface of varying length, configuration and degree of banking, but always with four left turns.

PPG Indy Car World Series
The entire schedule of Indy-car races, including the Indy 500. The National Championship is awarded on the basis of points earned for finishing positions. The series carries the name of its sponsor, PPG Industries Inc.

rpm
The number of revolutions the crankshaft of an engine makes in one minute. Cosworth engines make 11,400 rpm, or over two million revolutions during an Indy 500 race.

Sprint car
A solid-axle, open-wheel, single-seat race car with a wheelbase of at least 84 inches and no more than 90 inches, a front engine of 575 horsepower, and a minimum chassis weight of 1,400 pounds.

Super Vee Series
A series of races on either an oval or road course for open-wheel, single-seat, scaled-down versions of Indy-type cars. Cars use fuel-injected Volkswagen Scirocco engines with 190 to 200 horsepower and a chassis weighing 959 pounds. The series is considered an excellent training ground for Indy hopefuls.

USAC
United States Auto Club. The non-profit organization that sanctions and supervises the Indy 500 and other racing competitions in many types of cars, from midgets and sprints to Indy cars. USAC was founded in 1955 and establishes chassis and engine specifications for each division, and administers race rules.

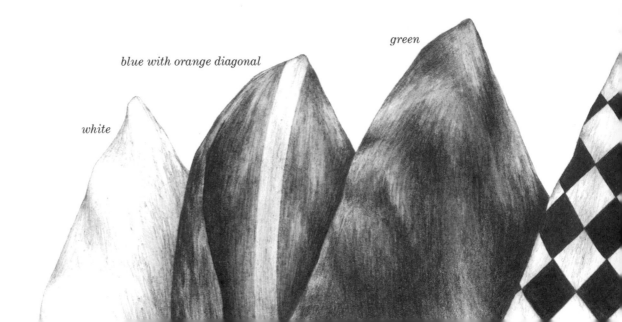

green

blue with orange diagonal

white

Photo Credits

Numbers indicate pages on which photographs appear. Letters refer to the placement of the photograph on the page, read from left to right, top to bottom.

James R. Alvis
250(a–f), 251(a–e)

Richard Chenet
36(b,f,l), 37(c), 170(a), 194–195, 200(c), 201(c), 227, 228–229

Jim Gilmore Enterprises.
97, 171

IMS Photography Staff
16, 34(g), 37(j,m), 45(d), 55(b), 56, 58–59, 62(a–f), 63(a–f), 66(a–d), 67, 68, 69(a,b), 70(a–d), 71(a–d), 72(a,b), 73, 74(a), 76–77, 78, 79, 80, 81, 82–83, 189(b), 202–203, 208(a,b), 209(b), 260, Mag Binkley 37(d), 103(b), Dave Dwiggins 36(k), Dan Francis 37(b), 100, 116(a,b), 172(b), 173(b), 238–239, Jim Haines 37(f), Harlen Hunter 232(a,b), 233, Steve Lingenfelter 32(c), 36(n), 37(k), 99(a,c), 149(a–d), 273(c), Tom Lucas 37(g), Ron McQueeney 106–107, 172(d), 173(c), 197, 198–199, 254(a), 269, Frank Newman 163(a), Tammie Phillips 94, 126, Mark Reed 262–263, 273(d), Jack Schafer 30(a), 33(a), Larry Seidman 174(a), 254(b), Lance Sellers 288, Larry Smith 209(a), Steve Snoddy 145, 200(a,d), 201(b), Leigh Spargur 37(e), Denis Sparks 35(g), Kay Totten Spivey 36(h), Jeff Stephenson 99(d), 240, Steve Swope 30(b), 32(a), 36(j), 152, 204(c), Bill Watson 37(l), 55(a), 98(e), 99(f), 104(a), Dave Willoughby 105, 115(a), Dale Wines 175(c), Debbie Young 98(d), 270(a–h), 271(a–h), Mike Young 35(e), 165(f).

Chet Jezierski
1, 2–3, 25, 26–27, 28, 29, 31(a,b), 32(b,d), 33(b), 34(a–e), 35(a,c,d,f), 36(a,c,e,g), 37(i), 38–39, 40, 50(a,b), 52–53, 86, 87, 90, 98(a,c,f), 99(e), 101(a,b), 102(a,b,d–g), 103(d–h), 114(a), 117, 122, 143(a,b), 150–151, 168(a,b), 172(a), 174(d), 176, 192(a,b), 193, 196(b), 204(a,b,d), 205, 206–207, 210–211, 225, 226(a,b), 230–231, 234–235, 236, 237(a,b), 261, 282–283, 286–287

Paul Kennedy/Sports Illustrated
35(h), 51, 189(a), 255

Heinz Kluetmeier/Sports Illustrated
188, 201(d), 212, 253(b), 256–257

Bill McGurk/Goodyear Tire & Rubber Company
36(m)

Ronald C. Modra/Sports Illustrated 258(a–d), 259(a–d)

Buck Miller/Sports Illustrated
249

Nick Nicholson
84, 123, 155(a), 181

Bill Stahl
4–5, 6–7, 8–9, 10–11, 12–13, 14–15, 33(c,d), 34(f,h), 35(b), 36(d,i,o,p), 37(n–p), 54, 75(d), 98(b), 99(b), 102(c,h), 103(a,c), 104(b), 108, 109(a,b), 110(a–d), 111(a–d), 112–113, 114(b), 115(b), 118–119, 120, 129, 130, 131(a,b), 132–133, 134, 135, 136–137, 138(a,b), 139, 140–141, 142, 144, 146(a–d), 147(a–d), 148(a–d), 154, 155(b), 156(a,b), 157, 159, 161, 162(a–h), 163(b–h), 164(a–h), 165(a–e,g,h), 166, 167(a–d), 169, 170(b), 172(c), 173(a,d), 174(b,c), 175(a,b,d), 182–183, 184(a,b), 185(a–p), 186–187, 190–191, 196(a), 200(b), 201(a), 223, 252(a,b), 253(a), 264, 272(a–d), 273(b), 274–275, 276, 281

George Tiedemann/Sports Illustrated
37(h), 273(a)

Robert Tronolone
37(a), 49, 61, 64, 65, 74(b–f), 75(a–c,e,f), 266, 284–285

Illustration Credits

Aerodynamics drawing, 178, courtesy Associated Press

Cotter Racing chart, 88–89, courtesy Cotter Racing

Flags, 278–279, drawn by Ayn Svoboda

Lola T-86/00, 216, courtesy Newman/Haas Racing

March 85C, 214, 219, courtesy March Engineering

Marlboro/Patrick March 86C, 220–221, courtesy Philip Morris Corp.

Patrick Racing chart, 93, courtesy Patrick Racing

Racing gear, 222, 223, 242–243, 246, courtesy Simpson Sports

Safety drawings, 244–245, courtesy The Physician and Sportsmedicine, May '86

Speedway map, 18–19, courtesy Indianapolis Motor Speedway Corp.

Unser family album, 42–43, 44–45(a–c, e–j), courtesy Marsha Unser

The Unsers at the White House, 46–47, courtesy The White House

USAC logo, 92, courtesy the United States Auto Club

Book Title

The trademark INDY 500™ is used by the author in the title of this book with permission of the Indianapolis Motor Speedway Corporation.

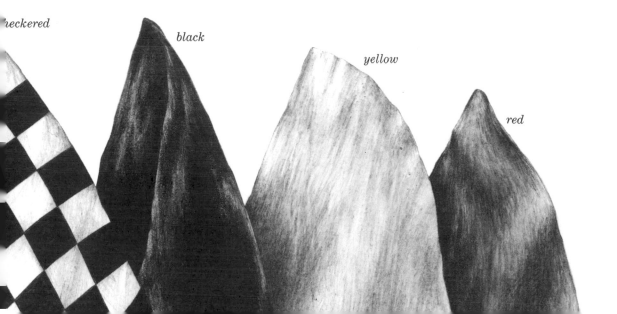

checkered   black   yellow   red

Index

Numbers in regular type refer to text. Numbers in italics refer to photographs.

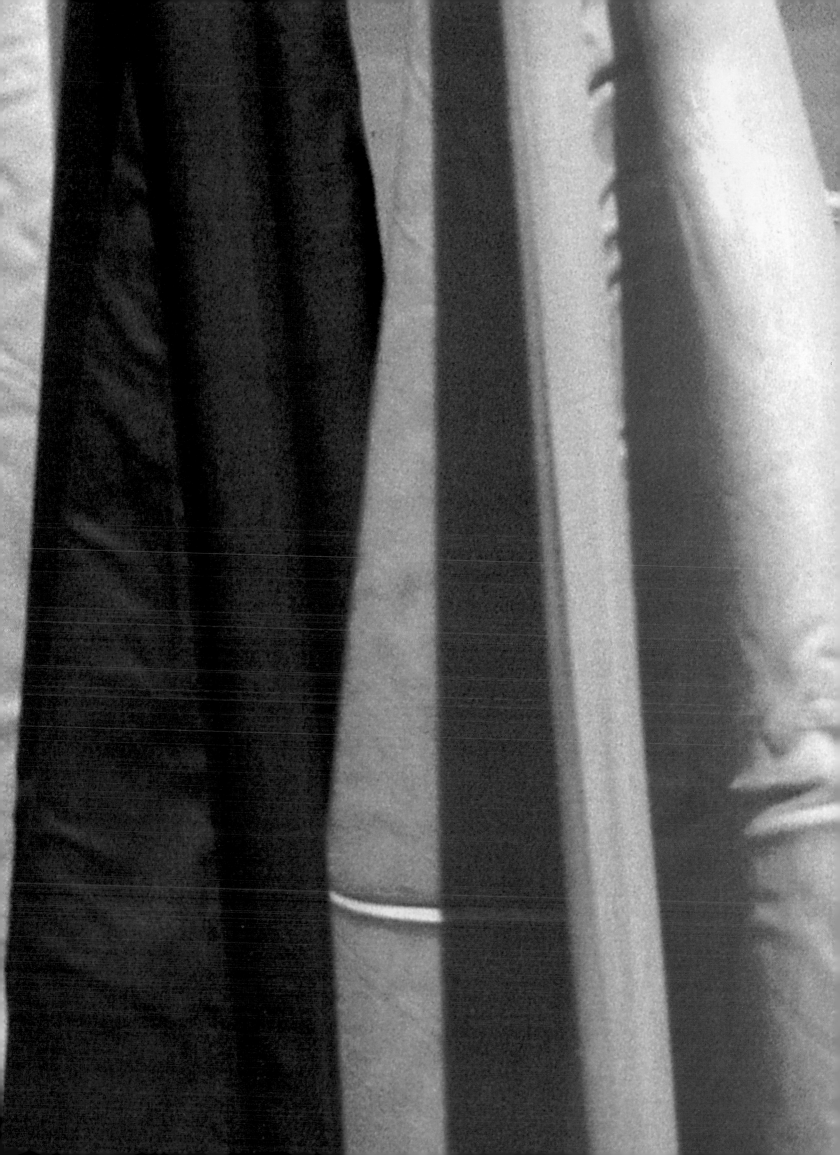

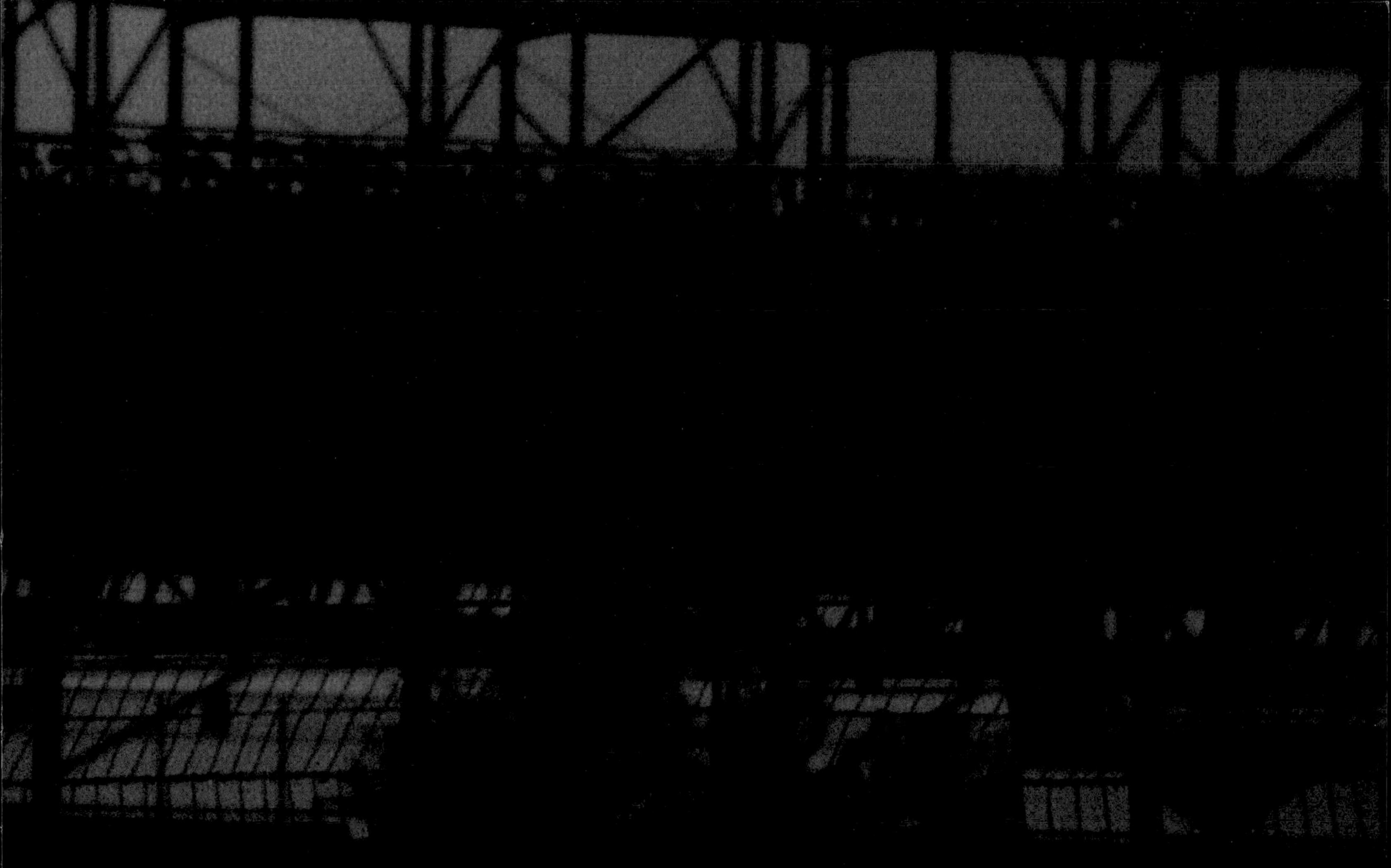